ACADEMIC RESEARCH, WRITING AND REFERENCING

PEARSON

We work with leading authors to develop the strongest
educational materials in study skills, bringing cutting-edge
thinking and best learning practice to a global market.

Under a range of well-known imprints, including Longman,
we craft high quality print and electronic publications
which help readers to understand and apply their content,
whether studying or at work.

To find out more about the complete range of our
publishing, please visit us on the World Wide Web at:
www.pearsoned.co.uk

INSIDE TRACK

ACADEMIC RESEARCH, WRITING AND REFERENCING

Dr Mary Deane

Centre for Academic Writing
Coventry University

Longman
is an imprint of

Harlow, England • London • New York • Boston • San Francisco • Toronto
Sydney • Tokyo • Singapore • Hong Kong • Seoul • Taipei • New Delhi
Cape Town • Madrid • Mexico City • Amsterdam • Munich • Paris • Milan

Pearson Education Limited
Edinburgh Gate
Harlow
Essex CM20 2JE
England

and Associated Companies throughout the world

Visit us on the World Wide Web at:
www.pearsoned.co.uk

First published 2010

ISBN: 978-1-4082-3698-7

British Library Cataloguing-in-Publication Data
A catalogue record for this book is available from the British Library

Library of Congress Cataloging-in-Publication Data
Deane, Mary.
    Academic reading, writing, and referencing / Mary Deane.
        p.   cm.
    ISBN 978-1-4082-3698-7 (pbk.)
  1. Reading.   2. Literacy.   3. Language arts.   I. Title.
    LB1573.D343   2010
    808'.02—dc22

                                                        2010005339

10 9 8 7 6 5 4 3 2 1
14 13 12 11 10

Typeset in 9/12.5 pt Helvetica Neue by 73
Printed in Great Britain by Henry Ling Limited, at the Dorset Press, Dorchester, DT1 1HD

This book is dedicated to Matt

CONTENTS

Part 4 REFERENCING

Contents

LIST OF FIGURES

LIST OF TABLES

FOREWORD

When I was asked to write the Foreword to *Academic Research, Writing and Referencing,* I expected that I would be endorsing a cleverly and precisely crafted work which was well suited to the needs of university students, in particular those encountering tertiary level research assignments for the first time. Given what I knew of Mary Deane's excellent work in the Centre for Academic Writing at Coventry University, I had no doubt that her succinct text would mirror the friendly, energetic, practical, and intellectually incisive personality she projects to colleagues in correspondence and at international conferences.

In fact, Mary Deane's book is the ideal guide for the new university student in the UK embarking on academic writing and research in classes across the disciplines. One of its great strengths is that it doesn't try to do too much – but what it sets out to do it does superbly.

This admirably concise text makes conscious and systematic the skills that successful scholars have learned over the years and made a tacit part of their practice. For example, her 'LARC' strategy (in Part 2 Research) gives students an easy-to-remember process for finding useful sources, quickly assessing their relevance, and, most important, reading them critically. It does all this with panache, crisp language, and visual flair: e.g. a text box states boldly:

> Sources should be:
> - Relevant
> - Readily available
> - Reliable.

and then goes on to illustrate each quality with brief descriptions and graphic lists of questions to guide the systematic researcher. Her clear voice is that of the skilled teacher, at once demanding excellence and understanding student difference:

> You should consider how savvy you are at present in your use of sources. If you are naturally sceptical you should apply this attribute to your selection and analysis of texts. If you are naturally naïve you should resist this tendency and develop an aptitude for critical reading to write with confidence and originality.

The author's ability to deliver good advice in a memorable way derives at least in part from her daily experience serving Coventry students in the university's innovative Centre for Academic Writing, one of a growing number in the UK, the US, and other countries around the world. Founded on the concept of 'Writing Across the Curriculum' (WAC), these centres recognise that students can learn to produce good academic writing by systematically learning the skills of scholarly researchers. Organisations such as the European Writing Centers Association (EWCA), the European Association of Teachers of Academic Writing (EATAW), and the International Network of Writing

Across the Curriculum Programs (INWAC) nurture the work of these centres by fostering collaboration in practices and research through their conferences and publications.

Staff in these centres recognise that qualities of successful academic writing vary by discipline, with the humanities, for example, valuing different methods and formats from those in the sciences. Deane's *Academic Research, Writing and Referencing,* meant for students with diverse disciplinary ambitions, concentrates on those skills and values that cut across all academic fields – while also showing students some differences in how writers from different disciplines use and cite sources. Chapters 10 and 11, for example, illustrate many aspects of the Harvard style of citation (Chapter 10), then show (Chapter 11) features of the MLA (humanities), APA (social sciences), and CSE (life and physical sciences) citation methods. The book, exemplifying the spirit of the Centre for Academic Writing, honours both those values that all disciplines share and those that distinguish them.

Two more emphases of the book stand out for me:

- Using non-print, especially web-based, resources
- Maintaining academic integrity in writing and research.

Throughout her chapters, Deane attends to the ubiquity of the internet in most students' lives. Rather than issue warnings against the use of web-based sources in research, she follows her pragmatic path of giving clear, succinct guidance in what to look for and what to avoid, how to assess, and how to cite. For example, she recommends three basic questions for website searchers to ask: 'Who is the author?' 'Are the contents attributed or acknowledged?' 'Who is the audience?' Her pithy explanations following each question demonstrate the savvy, critical researcher at work. Another case in point is her advice regarding Wikipedia. Rather than merely dismissing this erratically monitored tool, she acknowledges its coverage and convenience for 'getting started on a topic' – then gives readers a simple method for following through:

> To prevent yourself repeating errors you can check an alternative source, preferably a more scholarly one such as a textbook. If the information is corroborated, you can use it for your writing, but it is often preferable to borrow information from the more scholarly source and cite that in accordance with your chosen referencing style.

Deane's cautious, but appreciative, view of the convenience of digital tools in academic research writing comprises one of several threads in her thorough Part 1 Academic integrity. Perhaps most basic to these opening chapters is her understanding of the international, cross-cultural audience of students she is addressing. Although she reminds us that the setting is the UK university, her readers are not only those brought up in UK schools but also those who come from a wide range of nations and research traditions:

> The independence required of UK university students might put particular pressures on students, especially when working in a second language. Not all academic cultures demand student writers to advance their own arguments . . . clearly distinguished from, existing research.

She recommends that students avail themselves of the advice of their tutors and of 'short courses on research, reading, and writing' that their universities might offer – perhaps through their versions of academic writing centres.

In *Academic Research, Writing and Referencing,* Mary Deane has not written a book that she means to stand by itself as a guide to inexperienced student researchers, albeit its clarity, variety, and practicality. Rather, it will come fully to life in the hands of the student who augments its many, many useful tips with advice from tutors, librarians, and more savvy fellow students. For the teacher, it can be the book you recommend or that to which you turn for just the right tool or path to suggest to the new seeker of knowledge.

Chris Thaiss

Clark Kerr Presidential Chair, Professor, and Director, University Writing Program, University of California, Davis

Co-ordinator, International Network of Writing-across-the-Curriculum Programs

INTRODUCTION: ENTERING THE ACADEMY

The aim of this book is to foster your confidence in undertaking research, writing, and referencing at an advanced level. The explanations, examples, and quizzes are designed to help you to become a more organised and independent scholar so that you can enjoy studying and develop expertise in your chosen discipline.

This book is particularly valuable for writers in the Humanities and Social Sciences but the tips about locating, assessing, and reading sources apply more widely. The book is divided into four parts:

- Part 1 Academic integrity
- Part 2 Research
- Part 3 Writing
- Part 4 Referencing.

Part 1 introduces the culture of scholarly practice and points out that your academic success is in your own hands. By explaining academic integrity and ways of avoiding plagiarism, these topics are demystified to help you manage information effectively, plan your time, and keep complete records of your sources.

Part 2 explains the LARC research strategy. This stands for Locating, Assessing, and Reading Critically. Although these three stages of research are presented in a linear way, you should move back and forth between them as you select, reject, and evaluate sources. By proposing this systematic approach to research, the book shows you how to be savvy about using sources and stresses the value of starting research early, respecting your deadline, and keeping your purpose in sight.

Part 3 demonstrates how to integrate sources into your writing by quoting, paraphrasing, summarising, critiquing, and acknowledging your sources in a scholarly way. It suggests that these techniques should all be used in your academic writing to display agility and critical thinking as you draw upon research. It emphasises that all writing is indebted to existing ideas and that evaluating scholarship can help you contribute to knowledge.

Part 4 explores how to cite and reference in the Harvard style and discusses other referencing systems because the conventions are distinctive in each discipline. It explains that you need to check the recommended referencing style in your subject area and seek your tutors' advice. It recommends learning the conventions for citing and referencing in your field and practising until they become automatic.

Introduction: entering the academy

The main message of *Academic Research, Writing and Referencing* is that, with the practical and proactive approach outlined here, you can contribute to scholarly debates by discovering, extending, and generating knowledge. This book argues that the key to enhancing your academic performance is good time management, which will help you avoid plagiarism, research effectively, enjoy writing, and develop skill in referencing.

ABOUT THE AUTHOR

Dr Mary Deane is a Senior Lecturer in Academic Writing at Coventry University's Centre for Academic Writing. She specialises in writing development, academic practice, publication strategies, rhetorical theory, and digital media for learning and teaching.

ACKNOWLEDGEMENTS

I would like to thank Moira and Pat Deane for their generosity and support.

I wish to thank Steve Temblett, Katy Robinson, and Mary Lince of Pearson Education for their expertise. I would also like to thank Sarah Beanland, Loulou Brown, and Kate Legon for their work on this book.

I am grateful to my colleagues at the Centre for Academic Writing for their great help: Catalina Neculai, Clare Panter, Cynthia Barnes, Dimitar Angelov, Erik Borg, Holly Vass, Janet Collinge, Jon Morley, Lisa Ganobcsik-Williams, Magda Ciepalowicz, Miriam Evans, Monica Sharma, Penny Gilchrist, Phil Russell, Ray Summers, Sarah Wilkerson, Sheila Medlock, and Tom Parkinson.

I extend warm thanks to Mollie Howell-Joynson, Emma and Jenny Joynson, Josie Facchetti, Paul Grove, Teresa and Tim Fediw, Charley and Tom Gaston, Joe and Paul Deane, Mad and Andrew Bastawrous, Berne Fosberry, Gwen Dagorne, Emma McCormack, Sarah Dauncey, Nikki Martin, Dorothy Baker, Zak John, Ness and Jasmine Burchell, Pat and Bill Lyness, Paul, Kathy, Joe, Emily, Ben and Isabelle Lyness, Dave, Jasmine, Isabella and Sally Jackson, Simon Bell, Steve Foster, and Hammad Qureshi.

I am indebted to Chris Thaiss, Cinthia Gannett, John Brereton, Tiane Donahue, and Trevor Day for their advice.

PUBLISHER'S ACKNOWLEDGEMENTS

We are grateful to the following for permission to reproduce copyright material:

Figures
Figure 10.3 from Effective Writing and Referencing, http://studyingeconomics.ac.uk/effective-writing/, The Economics Network of the Higher Education Academy, University of Bristol. Thanks to Jonathan Pinder and Miriam Best of the Economics Network; Figure 10.4 from *Successful Academic Writing,* Pearson Education (Gillett, A., Hammond, A. and Martala, M. 2009) front cover.

Text
Extracts on pages 20, 74, 75, 77, 92, 94, 95 and 100, reprinted from Understanding 'Internet Plagiarism', *Computers and Composition,* 24 (1), pp. 3–15 (Howard, R.M. 2007), with permission from Elsevier; extract on pages 64–5 from Personality, social relationships, and vocational indecision among college students: the mediating

effects of identity construction, *Career Development International,* 14 (4), 309–32 (Ng, T.W.H. and Feldman, D.C. 2009), © Emerald Group Publishing Limited all rights reserved; extracts on pages 101, 102 and 103 reprinted from 'It wasn't me, was it?' Plagiarism and the web, *Computers and Composition,* 19 (2), pp. 191–203 (DeVoss, D. and Rosati, A.C. 2002), with permission from Elsevier.

In some instances we have been unable to trace the owners of copyright material, and we would appreciate any information that would enable us to do so.

PART 1

ACADEMIC INTEGRITY

INTRODUCTION TO PART 1

Part 1 provides tips on succeeding at an advanced level by explaining the expectations of scholarly practice. Chapter 1 defines academic integrity and discusses how to display integrity as you select sources and follow the conventions of your discipline. Chapter 2 defines plagiarism and explains how to avoid it by managing your time effectively and adopting scholarly practice.

AVOID PLAGIARISM BY KEEPING FULL RECORDS

Before reading Part 1, you should think about the types of sources you might need to find, read, and critique for your written assessments and consider the information you need to record about these types of sources (Williams and Carroll 2009: 8). Make notes not just about the sources, but also about the author, date, and publication information to avoid plagiarising. Here is a list of the main details to record for in-text citations:

- Note the surname of authors
- Note the date of publication or the revised date if applicable
- Note the *page numbers* for images, data, or ideas in printed sources which you may want to borrow for your own work.

If you forget to record any of these details you will waste time hunting for sources, and if you cannot locate materials again your in-text citations will be incomplete so you will be vulnerable to charges of plagiarism as discussed in Chapter 1.

For the list of references:

- Ensure you have the surname and initials of the authors
- Ensure you have the date of publication or the revised date
- Note the title of chapters, articles, webpages, etc.
- Note the title of books, journals, reports, websites, etc.
- Note the place of publication for printed sources
- Note the publisher for printed sources
- Note the volume and part or issue number (if relevant) for journals
- Note the full website address (URL) when you access sources online
- Note the date of access when you visit sites online or download sources
- Note the first and last page numbers for chapters in books and articles in journals, newspapers, magazines, etc.

Make the effort to develop a routine of recording this information and, after a short time, it will become easy and automatic. Citing and referencing will also become clearer the more you practise and get feedback from your tutors. Remember that the time you invest in adopting scholarly methods will be well worth it, because developing a systematic and professional approach to research, writing, and referencing can enhance your academic performance.

TYPES OF SOURCES

As writing requirements are distinctive in each discipline you may not require all the types listed below, but you should be aware that research at an advanced level demands that you consult a wide range of sources to generate your own ideas about the topics you are studying (Williams and Carroll 2009: 9).

Written sources

Most writers borrow material from written sources every time they prepare a written assessment, and scholarly writers acknowledge all their sources using an appropriate referencing style. Here are some examples of written sources:

- Books
- Journal articles
- Reports
- Surveys and questionnaires
- Newspaper articles
- Magazine articles
- Song lyrics.

Numerical sources

Scholarly writers acknowledge all the statistics, calculations, and other sorts of numerical data they borrow for their writing. Here are some examples of numerical sources:

- Statistics
- Mathematical calculations
- Computer programs.

Audiovisual sources

Scholarly writers also acknowledge all the audio and visual data they borrow for their writing. Here are some examples:

- Television programmes
- Films
- Recordings of interviews
- Recordings of lectures
- Paintings
- Sculptures
- Photographs
- Graphics
- Diagrams
- Graphs
- Figures
- Tables.

FORMATS

Many sources are available digitally and, although this can be an advantage by making them easy to access, it is essential to evaluate digital sources before using them for your academic writing. Scholarly writers check the relevance and appropriateness of digital media before selecting them as source material. When you access sources online make sure you record the website address (URL) and the date you viewed or downloaded material (called the date of access). You will need these details for your referencing. Here are some examples of digital sources you might access online:

- Websites
- Electronic books
- Electronic journals
- Listservs and discussion groups
- Email correspondence
- Podcasts.

Part 1 is designed to enhance your independence, confidence, and effectiveness as a scholar by explaining the culture of scholarly practice. The main message of the following two chapters is that academic success is in your own hands, and with a proactive approach to advanced level study you can maximise your academic success.

1 ▶ ACADEMIC INTEGRITY

This chapter introduces the concept of academic integrity and discusses how to acknowledge all your sources with clarity and consistency. It emphasises that academic conventions can vary in different disciplines and explains that you need to familiarise yourself with the norms in your subject area.

The chapter covers:

- Scholarly practice
- Advancing knowledge
- Selecting sources
- Academic conventions
- Seeking support.

Using this chapter

WHAT IS ACADEMIC INTEGRITY?

Academic integrity means being explicit about where you have borrowed ideas, images, and data for your writing at university. This transparency in acknowledging sources shows your regard for the standards scholars are expected to uphold and demonstrates your professionalism as an academic writer (Howard 2007: 13). The important advantage of crediting others is that this also enables you to highlight your own ideas (Neville 2007: 9).

Academic integrity signals your trustworthiness to readers, who are more likely to be convinced by your arguments if you come across as an honest writer (Lunsford 2009: 191). This is especially significant when you are writing for assessment because credit is given for convincing arguments based on evidence and critical thinking (Hacker 2006: 30).

There are four main aspects of academic integrity that you should be aware of as you develop strategies for effective research, writing, and documentation of the sources you draw upon for your studies. These are:

1 Academic standards
2 Academic conventions
3 Academic code of practice
4 Advancing knowledge.

Academic standards

Advanced level study requires you to uphold high standards of academic practice when you undertake research or produce written assessments. You must be transparent about your influences of every kind and respect the intellectual property of other writers, artists, or researchers. You show this respect by citing and referencing your sources according to the advice given to you by tutors and the tips in this book. These might include digital media, books, and journal articles you have read and referred to in your writing.

Selecting sources

You also meet academic standards by selecting your sources with care and ensuring that they are relevant to the purpose of your writing (Lunsford 2009: 170). The authors' credentials must match the intellectual level demanded by advanced level study because inadequate source material can hinder your chances of academic success. To select appropriate scholarly material you need to develop both proficiency in using your university library and expertise in finding sources via the relevant databases for your subject area (Hacker 2006: 6).

Academic conventions

The conventions for acknowledging other people's intellectual property tend to vary in different academic disciplines, so you need to familiarise yourself with the practice in your field (Williams and Carroll 2009: 9). In addition to the guidance provided by your tutors, you can pick up a wealth of information by reading scholarly journal articles about the topics you are studying, especially those recommended by your tutors. Relevant journal articles can be informative not only owing to the contents, but also because they adhere to disciplinary conventions for written expression and textual organisation. On the other hand, you should be aware that journals and publishers have their own style for citing and referencing sources, so you should take advice from your tutors rather than emulating the documentation styles adopted in the sources you read. Follow the system your tutors recommend for in-text citations and your list of references:

- Be *clear* when documenting sources
- Be *consistent* when documenting sources
- Be *complete* when documenting sources.

SCHOLARLY PRACTICE

Although the practicalities of researching, writing, and referencing are distinctive in each context, there is a code of academic practice that is applicable across the disciplines. Scholarly practice is expressed in different ways within institutions but, in essence, you are expected to be professional in all the written assessments you produce. Scholarly practice means producing quality work that is independently generated except where you acknowledge borrowed material or the contributions of others. Here are some other ways of enhancing your success:

- Plan ahead
- Be an independent scholar
- Produce high quality work
- Learn how to cite and reference in your discipline
- Acknowledge borrowed material and contributions from others
- Read widely and make comprehensive notes
- Attend classes regularly and participate fully
- Prepare for examinations
- Practise past examination papers.

Scholarly practice demands that you research widely to develop your knowledge about topics. It means making careful notes when you are reading or attending lectures so you can acknowledge sources in your writing. It also involves learning how to cite and reference in the style required by your tutors. Crucially, scholarly practice implies managing your time efficiently and working independently.

In the case of examinations, scholarly practice involves being prepared for questions by taking part in classes regularly and keeping up with the work. This kind of proactive approach to study includes making a revision timetable, covering the material on your syllabus, and practising using exam papers from previous years. Adopting scholarly practice can maximise your chances of success and enable you to develop transferable skills such as the ability to analyse and apply information, which will be highly valued by your future employers.

Seeking support

Universities assure the quality of all students' scholarly practice by setting written assessments and examinations which test students' ability to think for themselves based on the material they have studied. If you are concerned about any aspect of your studies you should speak to your tutor, specialists in your university library, or other staff at your institution, because there are systems in place to support students who are new to independent research, writing, and referencing at an advanced level.

New to university

Students who make the transition to university often find it hard to adopt a more independent style of study. The key is to seek advice from tutors and to learn how to adopt scholarly practice by reading study guides like this book as well as examples of scholarship in your field, including books and journal articles (Williams and Carroll 2009: 3).

New to university in the UK

Students who travel to the UK to undertake advanced level study may have to learn how to adopt certain aspects of scholarly practice. The independence required of UK university students might put particular pressures on students, especially when working in a second language. Not all academic cultures demand student writers to advance their own arguments based on, yet clearly distinguished from, existing research (Neville 2007: 31, Lunsford 2008: 284). Understanding this fundamental aspect of scholarly practice and knowing how to fulfil it takes time, practice, and, most of all, feedback from tutors on how to improve.

If you are new to studying in the UK, you should make contact with your tutors and ask them to recommend sources you can consult to enhance your scholarly practice. Also enquire at your university whether there are any short courses on research, reading, or writing strategies. This is particularly important if you are unfamiliar with the requirement to cite and reference all the sources to which you refer in your writing. Whether or not you are familiar with UK scholarly codes of practice, you will be penalised for failing to acknowledge all the sources from which you borrow ideas, images, or data of any kind (Williams and Carroll 2009: 52).

ADVANCING KNOWLEDGE

Reading widely and acknowledging your sources is an excellent way to advance your own knowledge and understanding by engaging with other people's ideas (Howard 2007: 13). As indicated above, when you borrow *ideas* from sources you must cite and reference them. Similarly, when you borrow *words* from sources you must cite and reference them because both the **content** and the **expression** are the intellectual property of the author (Williams and Carroll 2009: 5). However, you should aim to use other people's intellectual property as a springboard to finding your own arguments. You may agree or disagree with the arguments you read, but either way your exposure to intellectual debate can spark new thoughts and insights.

Accurate citation and referencing can enable you to build upon existing research by outlining what others have argued and then applying the ideas in different contexts or offering your own perspective (Sopure *et al.* 1998: 410). This extension and re-application of knowledge is the most challenging aspect of scholarly practice, but it is also the most valorised in academia (DeVoss and Rosati 2002: 199). Being able to make your own contribution as you cite and reference sources reveals your standing as a scholar in your own right.

For many of your written assessments, tutors will encourage you to demonstrate critical thinking and the ability to form your own perspectives about the topics you are studying. Depending on your written task, the criteria against which you are assessed may also stipulate that originality is highly rewarded by markers. If you find this daunting, remember that research is the route to developing new ideas as long as you distinguish clearly between what you think and what others have already argued. Do not worry if you happen to read an idea that you had already thought of. If this happens, you should cite and reference the relevant source and, if possible, take time to develop your own idea more fully or offer some comment on the point as you acknowledge it.

SUMMARY

This chapter has introduced the concept of academic integrity and discussed the requirement for writers to acknowledge all their sources with clarity and consistency. It has stressed that academic conventions can vary in different disciplines and identified the need to familiarise yourself with the norms in your subject area. The chapter has explored the culture of advanced level study and started to unpack the nature of scholarly practice, which is further discussed in the following chapter alongside plagiarism and how to avoid it.

The main arguments in this chapter:

- Writing at an advanced level demands academic integrity
- This implies meeting high academic standards

- Academic conventions differ in each subject area
- Students new to university or new to university in the UK should become familiar with the culture and conventions of their field.

QUIZ

Read the extract below from an article by Kendall (2008) called 'The Assignment Sheet Mystery'. It is about students' use of assignment briefs (these are called assignment sheets in North America). Then read the two examples and decide which writer demonstrates academic integrity most effectively.

The Assignment Sheet Mystery

In order to learn how to compose in the discourse of the university community, students must include assignment sheets [briefs] as a critical component of the planning process. Such analysis is important because assignment sheets complicate the student writer's rhetorical situations – assignment sheets are texts written by teachers for the students, who are the readers (audience) and must negotiate between this text and that of the text they are asked to compose. Bawarshi claims that the writing prompt, like any other genre, 'organizes and generates the conditions within which individuals perform their activities' (2003: 127).

Most importantly, though, the analysis of assignment sheets should be incorporated into the planning process because students often misunderstand assignment sheets, as well as struggle with them. One reason for this struggle is that the students may not understand the language of the assignment sheet (Harris 1995: 38). Students may also become overwhelmed by particular verbs in the sheets, such as *analyze* and *compare* (Harris 1995: 39).

(Kendall 2008: 3)

Example 1

Interpreting assignment briefs is a significant part of writing at university, and when planning to write an assignment it is essential to read the instructions with care (Bawarshi). Analysing assignment briefs is important because it is easy to misinterpret assignment briefs owing to the complex language. Nevertheless, writers should dedicate part of the planning process to de-coding assignment briefs and think about the meaning of key words (Kendall 2008).

Example 2

Interpreting assignment briefs is a significant part of writing at university, and when planning to write an assignment it is essential to read the instructions with care (Kendall 2008: 3). Analysing assignment briefs is important because it is easy to misinterpret assignment briefs owing to the complex language (Harris 1995: 38 cited in Kendall 2008: 3). Nevertheless, writers should dedicate part of the planning process to de-coding assignment briefs and think about the meaning of key words (Kendall 2008: 3).

2   AVOIDING PLAGIARISM

This chapter suggests ways of maintaining academic integrity, including the KnACK strategy for avoiding plagiarism. This strategy entails **Kn**owing what you are doing, **A**cknowledging your sources, **C**reating your own perspectives, and being prepared to **K**eep revising your position to strengthen the originality of your work. This chapter highlights the importance of effective time management and suggests why some students plagiarise so you can avoid common pitfalls and improve your own chances of academic success.

The chapter covers:

- Defining plagiarism
- Avoiding plagiarism
- Time management
- A positive approach to citing and referencing
- Penalties for plagiarism.

Using this chapter

INTRODUCTION

Having introduced the concept of academic integrity, this chapter defines plagiarism and provides tips on avoiding unintentional plagiarism.

WHAT IS PLAGIARISM?

Plagiarism is the omission of acknowledgements when you borrow ideas, images, statistics, or other data from sources, or the attempt to present the intellectual property of another person as your own (Neville 2007: 28). Marsh (2004) offers the following comment about definitions of plagiarism as a negative act:

> Most generic plagiarism definitions – drawing on the Latin *plagium* ('net to entangle game') – stress that plagiarism is stealing, kidnapping, or theft of intellectual property.
>
> (Marsh 2004: 428)

Although plagiarism is penalised at university, learning how to avoid it also represents a chance to learn ways of improving your research and writing so, rather than focusing on problems you might encounter, try concentrating on the opportunity to learn new strategies for generating and disseminating knowledge in a scholarly fashion (Howard 2007: 13).

A positive approach

Many writers worry about plagiarism and find that this stress has a negative impact on their experience of university or their academic performance. While it is important to adopt the codes of academic practice outlined in the introduction, the more you enjoy discovering information and generating your own ideas, the less likely you are to plagiarise unintentionally.

Although you may not be aware of it, you make decisions about whether or not to plagiarise all the time; for instance, by reading this book you are choosing to learn about scholarly practice to prevent plagiarism in your work. So, you can relax to some extent because you are raising your game academically by seeking this guidance. Build upon this excellent start by thinking about your written assessments for yourself and acknowledging all the ideas, information, images, statistics, and other data from which you borrow for your own writing.

DEVELOPING A <u>KnACK</u> FOR AVOIDING PLAGIARISM

Learning how to avoid plagiarism takes patience and perseverance, especially if this approach to research and writing is new to you. The opposite of plagiarising is generating new knowledge, and the tips below help you to make this your priority. The simple way to avoid plagiarism is to produce your own work and credit the work of others using an appropriate system for citing and referencing sources. More specifically, you can avoid accidental plagiarism by focusing on what you know or think about the subject you are discussing in your writing.

Here are four tips to help you get the KnACK for generating ideas of your own:

1 **Kn**ow what you are doing for each written assessment

2 **A**cknowledge your sources

3 **C**reate your own perspective based upon research

4 **K**eep revising your position to strengthen the originality of your work.

Often, the difference between a writer who plagiarises accidentally and one who does not, is the evidence of the latter's thought processes, which reveal to readers that the work is original. Following the KnACK approach to generating ideas will help you deepen your knowledge so you can make this learning apparent in your writing and receive the credit you are due when examiners give you feedback (Neville 2007: 12).

Know what you are doing for each written assessment

Unless you understand the task you have been set or the steps involved in completing your research project, it is impossible to carry it out successfully. Knowing what you need to do is therefore the first step to success and this is where you need to start generating ideas. Read any guidance you have been given and take time to brainstorm about the various ways you could tackle your task. Seek further advice if necessary, and, if appropriate, you could put together an initial plan and ask your tutor for comments.

Acknowledge your sources

At an advanced level it is unusual to receive a written assessment or to undertake work that does not draw on existing research, ideas, images, data, or information. Although it is not possible to generalise, tutors usually expect to see evidence of your research and acknowledgements within your writing each time you borrow material.

Create your own perspective based upon research

The advantage of taking this scholarly approach is that it enables you to isolate the intellectual property of others from your own thinking. As readers and examiners are mostly interested in your assessment of the subject, developing a knack for building on what others have argued is one route to academic success. So, whenever it is appropriate, try to use your acknowledgement of sources as a stepping stone to positing your own ideas.

Keep revising your position to strengthen the originality of your work

The generation of new perspectives and insights takes time, and unless you allow yourself the opportunity to refine your thinking you can undermine your chances of success. Talking about and jotting down your ideas are essential to finding ways of articulating them clearly and organising them for the highest impact upon readers. Therefore, revising your position about a subject is an important part of generating new ideas and this may allow you to make a contribution to knowledge in your field.

TIME MANAGEMENT

Effective time management is essential to avoiding plagiarism (DeVoss and Rosati 2002: 194). Do not make the mistake of ignoring your project if it is unclear from the start, and do not expect your tutors to respond to last minute queries. You can take advantage of your tutor's office hours or ask questions during classes if you need clarification about the purpose of your task, but remember that academics are extremely busy and may not receive your message in time to respond before the deadline. Moreover, advanced level study requires you to take responsibility for your own study and to plan ahead, so be aware that if you delay in getting started with your work it is not your tutor's role to accommodate this lack of organisation.

On the other hand, there are structures in place at every institution to support students who require advice about study skills, welfare, and any issues that affect their chances of academic success. Find out about the systems in place at your own university by enquiring at the library, the Students' Union, or other units such as the Disabilities Office, the Welfare Office, and the Academic Office. If you take steps to help yourself you will be well supported, but it is up to you to seek the advice you need to work effectively.

Tutors expect you to locate the sources they recommend on reading lists and in other documents, so you need to plan ahead to access books and journals at the earliest opportunity. This is especially true if colleagues may be seeking the same texts as you, and if you leave your research to the last minute you could be disadvantaged from the outset by a lack of relevant material.

However, if you do find yourself in this situation, try finding an electronic version of the books you need to read. Although search engines (such as Google™, for instance) can be problematic because they provide access to inaccurate, misleading, and unscholarly material, they also give you access to scholarly sources. Search for books you have been recommended via an online forum (for example, Amazon) and you can probably read useful extracts for your writing. Remember to record all the information you need to acknowledge the source in your chosen referencing style, including the page numbers. Record e-books in the appropriate format with the website address and the date you accessed the source.

Penalties for plagiarism

The two main categories of plagiarism are intentional and unintentional, and there are serious penalties for both kinds. A distinction is not necessarily made between these two categories because students are responsible for adopting scholarly practice and are expected to produce their own work to gain qualifications.

The penalties for plagiarism are set by individual institutions and these are usually outlined in the appropriate place on the university website and in the documentation distributed to students when they start a course. If you are unfamiliar with the penalties at your institution it is up to you to find out what they are, because they apply to you whether or not you know them in detail.

Depending on the extent and nature of a case of plagiarism, the penalties might include a mark of zero for an assignment, the outcome of fail for a course, or exclusion from the university. There are procedures in place at every university to give students who are suspected of plagiarism a fair hearing, and you can usually find this information listed under 'academic integrity', 'academic conduct', 'plagiarism', or related terms on your institution's website.

The main forms of plagiarism are shown in the box below (Neville 2007: 28).

Forms of plagiarism

Intentional plagiarism

- Omitting in-text citations in your writing
- Omitting sources in your list of references
- Omitting the list of references
- Taking material written by another person and submitting it as your own work
- Collusion, or co-writing an assignment with another person and submitting it as your own work
- Cheating in exams
- Purchasing an assignment on the internet and submitting it as your own work
- Attempting to gain credit for the same work twice by re-submitting all or part of a written assessment.

Unintentional plagiarism

- Inaccurate or incomplete in-text citations
- Inaccurate or incomplete list of references
- Poor quoting
- Poor paraphrasing
- Poor summarising.

Why study?

What is your main purpose for undertaking a degree? Is it to enhance your intellectual development generally, to learn about a new field specifically, to improve your chances of success professionally, or to enjoy the university environment? If you plagiarise either on purpose or by accident you are likely to undermine your purpose for studying, and you could also mar your academic record for the future. Howard (2007) asserts the importance of learning and points out that plagiarism undermines this activity:

> [P]lagiarism in the academy matters so dearly because writing assignments are intended to help students learn course materials and gain communication and thinking skills. If those assignments are undermined through plagiarism, none of that learning takes place, and the academic enterprise is itself endangered.
>
> (Howard 2007: 11)

The requirement to document sources explicitly and accurately is usually a feature of assessment criteria because tutors expect to see evidence of independent research. When critical thinking is a required part of an assessment, critiquing clearly documented sources is also valued. So, remember to incorporate acknowledged sources into your writing because this is the foundation upon which academic work is built.

WHY DO SOME WRITERS PLAGIARISE?

Reasons for unintentional plagiarism

There are many reasons why writers plagiarise by accident; for instance, they may lack confidence when it comes to documenting sources fully, or they may be unfamiliar with the conventions of research writing in their field (Neville 2007: 30).

Incomplete records

A common reason why writers plagiarise unintentionally is that they forget to record all the details necessary to cite and reference properly. It is much easier to keep notes as you go along than to hunt for sources at the last minute, so be organised and keep a record of the details you will need (Williams and Carroll 2009: 22).

Learn how to cite and reference the main types of sources you use and keep a manual or guide handy for the less common types of sources. Remember that documenting sources in your academic writing requires you to use your common sense when you encounter a source that you do not know how to reference. In this situation ask yourself whether it could be a variant on the format for a book, journal article, or website, and reference it in a clear and consistent manner.

Lacking confidence

Some writers plagiarise unintentionally because they are not sure how to cite and reference properly. If you are not clear about what to do, you are more likely to make unintentional errors, and the way to avoid this is to dedicate time to practising, and to take every opportunity to gain feedback from your tutors. You can also avoid accidental plagiarism by working with a friend and swapping texts to help each other spot omissions and errors. Often we cannot see our own mistakes, but we can easily identify problems in other people's work, so it can be invaluable to find a colleague and help each other out. Remember that collusion, or co-writing a piece of work that you submit as your own, is a form of plagiarism so only include your own ideas in your written assessments and credit the intellectual property you borrow from sources.

A different approach

Writers who travel to an English-speaking nation for their higher education may encounter a different approach to research and writing than that to which they are accustomed (Lunsford 2008: 284). Remember that acknowledging sources allows writers to build upon research to articulate their own ideas, which is valued very highly at English-speaking higher education institutions. If you need some tips, read the instructions you receive from your tutors and take advantage of training courses offered by the library, for instance, and if you have specific questions you should ask your tutor.

Similarly, writers who have recently started a higher education degree may find the conventions different from their previous experience. Not all schools and colleges require students to use referencing systems, and it can be very confusing at first. The best way to become more familiar with the conventions you should adopt at university is to read journal articles in your field. The added advantage is that journal articles show you how to present a scholarly argument based on evidence. Scholarly articles are superb examples of how to organise the shape and contents of advanced level writing, and in addition you will learn about your topic as you read.

Reasons for intentional plagiarism

There are also many reasons why writers plagiarise on purpose; for example, they may have poor time management skills or they might lack commitment to a course.

Time

Writers who are under the pressure of time sometimes choose to cheat by copying material without crediting the sources. There is no excuse for this, especially as the situation can be avoided by planning ahead. Although some people think that no one will notice, academics are expert at tracing the line of argument and analysing the style of texts so it is very easy for them to spot irregularities, differences in tone, and material taken from elsewhere. Plagiarism detection services such as Turnitin™ can identify use of unacknowledged material by scanning the contents and checking this against a comprehensive database of sources and academic assignments. For an informative critique of such services, see Marsh (2004).

Lacking commitment

Some writers do not appreciate the need to engage with the culture of scholarly writing and attributing ideas to authors. However, these are essential abilities to cultivate, and without learning how to research and reference effectively writers are unlikely to pass their courses. Some students do not realise that, in addition to the formal penalties for plagiarism, other consequences stem from not acknowledging sources:

- It obscures your efforts to search for relevant sources
- It hides the time you spend selecting sources
- It undermines your efforts to read and understand sources.

AVOIDING UNINTENTIONAL PLAGIARISM

You can avoid plagiarising unintentionally by displaying academic integrity as you research, write, and reference written assessments, reports, studies, and other kinds of academic work. Here are some tips to help you adopt a scholarly approach throughout your studies:

Tips on avoiding plagiarism

Research

- Do not forget to take full notes recording the details necessary to document your sources properly
- Jot down the page numbers for passages you may quote, paraphrase, or summarise
- Also note the page numbers for images, statistics, or other data you might borrow.

Writing

- Always introduce the ideas, images, data, and words you have borrowed from sources
- When appropriate, comment on the sources you integrate into your own writing
- Give page numbers as appropriate (when you refer to a specific page)
- Check your paraphrasing of passages is accurate
- Check your summarising of passages is accurate.

Referencing

- Learn how to use a reference management system such as EndNote or RefWorks
- Cite sources as you are writing in accordance with the recommended referencing style
- Give full details for each source you have cited in the list of references at the end of your work in accordance with the recommended referencing style
- Ask a friend to check your in-text citations and list of references.

WHAT DOES *NOT* REQUIRE REFERENCING?

There is an element of judgement involved in deciding when you need to acknowledge sources in your academic writing and when you do not (Neville 2007: 20). If you are unsure it is preferable to include an in-text citation rather than omit one in case you accidentally plagiarise a source. The conventions are distinct within disciplinary contents and, to help you learn about the practice in your field, you should read the texts your tutors have recommended. Notice in particular how authors do not document common knowledge or generally accepted facts (Lunsford 2009: 190). Here is a list of the types of material you do not usually need to cite and reference:

- Your own ideas
- Your own work
- General knowledge.

Your own ideas

You do not usually need to document your own ideas because they are your intellectual property. However, if you are unsure you should check this with your tutor because there may be exceptions. For instance, if you refer to work you have published or submitted for assessment already, it could be important for examiners to know this because an attempt to gain credit for the same piece of work twice is viewed as plagiarism.

Your own work

If you undertake research involving experimentation, data collection, or the generation of results you do not usually need to document your findings, providing the material is your own intellectual property. If you report the views or ideas of others, for instance through interviews or focus groups, you should acknowledge their contributions although this can be done anonymously. Follow the guidelines for ethical research practices at your institution and seek specific advice from tutors or expert researchers in your field.

General knowledge

If you refer to common knowledge, such as the dates of world wars, well known myths, or well established facts, you do not usually need to document the source because general knowledge implies a general holding of the intellectual property. On the other hand, if you refer to an author or artist's interpretation of a story or event, this is the intellectual property of another person and it must be acknowledged with accurate citation and referencing.

SUMMARY

This chapter has suggested ways of maintaining academic integrity, including the KnACK strategy for avoiding plagiarism which entails **Kn**owing what you are doing, **A**cknowledging your sources, **C**reating your own perspective, and being prepared to **K**eep revising your position to strengthen the originality of your work. The chapter has highlighted the importance of effective time management and outlined potential reasons for plagiarising so you can avoid these pitfalls and improve your own chances of academic success.

The main arguments in this chapter:

- You can take a positive and practical approach to avoiding plagiarism
- This takes time and forward planning
- It requires you to learn how to cite and reference
- It also takes practice.

QUIZ

1 Here is an extract from an article by Lawson et al. (2009) called 'Does the Multi-lateral Matter?' Is this passage missing any in-text citations?

Does the Multilateral Matter?

The International Monetary Fund (IMF), the World Bank and the World Trade Organization (WTO) have a common origin in the conference held in Bretton Woods, New Hampshire during July 1944 and share a focus on multilateral cooperation. But each addresses a different aspect of international economic interaction. The IMF and World Bank were created to address international monetary cooperation and development issues respectively.

(Lawson et al. 2009: 2)

---

2 Read the examples below and decide whether the writers were correct to document this information.

Example 1

As part of her study, the author took the photograph in Figure 1 to illustrate the behaviour of cats.

Figure 1: Cats' involvement in human activities
(Long 2010).

Example 2

An increased consumption of calories with no additional exercise results in weight gain (Edwards 2010).

Example 3

The story of Cinderella is a well known fairytale (Grimm and Grimm 1812) which has long been popular.

Example 4

Scholars have argued that leadership is a quality possessed by everyone, and external conditions determine whether or not individuals fulfil their potential (Potterson 2008, Zinger 2010).

PART 2
RESEARCH

INTRODUCTION TO PART 2

Part 2 introduces the LARC research strategy: this stands for Locating, Assessing, and Reading Critically. LARC represents a systematic approach to searching for sources by keeping your purpose in mind and avoiding inappropriate sources. The LARC research strategy is flexible so you can experiment with the suggested techniques and adapt them to suit your own style of research.

Chapter 3 explores ways of locating sources by undertaking literature searches and considering the variety of materials you could choose to consult. Chapter 4 investigates ways of assessing sources before beginning to read in depth. Chapter 5 looks in more depth at reading sources critically by evaluating the use of evidence and the suitability for your purpose.

Before reading Part 2 you should consider how savvy you are at present in your use of sources. If you are naturally sceptical you should apply this attribute to your selection and analysis of texts. If you are naturally naive you should resist this tendency and develop an aptitude for critical reading to write with confidence and originality.

Part 2 is designed to break down the three main stages involved in researching a topic for your writing, but the research process is *not linear* so you should move back and forth between these steps of locating, assessing, and reading sources critically. You may find, for instance, that you locate just one source and read it before returning to find others, perhaps using the source's citations and references to focus your search. The main message of the following three chapters is that undertaking research is time-consuming, so you need to begin as soon as possible and keep your deadline and purpose in sight. Remember:

1 Be systematic in locating sources
2 Assess the value of sources before you start to read
3 Be critical in reading sources and prepare to integrate critique into your writing.

3 ▶ LOCATING SOURCES

This chapter stresses the importance of searching for sources systematically and invites you to consider the relevance, ready availability, and reliability of materials in relation to your topic. It also provides tips on effective time management as you search the literature in your subject area.

The chapter covers:

- Systematic searching for sources
- The relevance of sources
- The ready availability of sources
- The reliability of sources
- Literature searches
- Using your university library
- Moving from general to specific research.

Using this chapter

INTRODUCTION

Chapter 2 offered tips on avoiding plagiarism; Chapter 3 now highlights the need for a system to search for the sources you will use in your writing. It stresses the importance of understanding your purpose for writing and explains how to move from seeking general sources to finding specifically relevant materials.

A SYSTEM FOR SEARCHING

Although your approach will differ based on the purpose of each writing task, you can develop a system for locating potentially useful sources that is adaptable to each assignment (Hacker 2006: 6, Lunsford 2008: 258).

Sources should be:

- Relevant
- Readily available
- Reliable.

Relevance

The relevance of sources depends upon the content, style, author, and intended audience (Lunsford 2008: 252). The clearer you are about the aim, style, and format of your own work, the better equipped you will be to find the right kinds of texts for your purpose. Do not neglect to search for numerical data and images if these are also relevant. Begin your systematic approach to locating the right sources for your task by thinking about these three questions:

1 What is the scope of the source?
2 Is this relevant to my writing?
3 Should I just make a record of this source (using a referencing management system, on paper, or on file) and move on?

Readily available

Once you have learnt how to use the catalogue, databases, and resources readily available via your university library you will not be dependent upon the internet, which is only one way to access materials and will not necessarily yield relevant sources for your purpose (Hacker 2006: 10). The next phase in your systematic approach to searching for sources is to consider these three questions:

1 Is there a paper-based copy in my university library?
2 Do I need to order the source from another library or collection?
3 Is there a digital copy accessible via my university library website using the catalogue, databases, or search engines?

Reliability

Sources are reliable if they are accurate, well designed, and written by authors with the right credentials for your purpose (Hacker 2006: 23). Mostly you will need to refer to scholarly sources for your academic writing, so the material you select should be based on valid research. It is often preferable to consult peer-reviewed sources because they have been verified by experts in the field. The third stage in your systematic approach to searching is to address these questions:

1 Is the information in the source confirmed elsewhere?
2 Is the author qualified to produce the source?
3 Is the source intended for academic use?

Peer review

Peer review is a process designed to ensure the quality, reliability, and originality of published material. Tutors often expect you to locate sources that have been peer-reviewed, which means that expert readers evaluate material and provide feedback on the areas requiring improvement, expansion, or revision. Blind peer review is when feedback is supplied anonymously and this is considered to be a more rigorous form of assessment.

If you are not sure whether sources have been peer-reviewed you can ask for advice at your university library or consult your tutors. The challenge of accessing sources online is that sources distributed via this digital environment do not always undergo peer review, and consequently they can be poorly phrased, badly organised or inaccurate. Therefore, do not rely exclusively on sources you have accessed online and instead research scholarly materials which have been assessed by experts and identified as reliable for academic use (Hacker 2006: 24–6).

RELEVANT SOURCES

When you receive an assignment brief or writing project, one of your first tasks is to analyse the requirements and begin to search for sources to help you fulfil your brief. It is often necessary to do independent research, and most often you will not be able to carry out the task successfully without drawing on existing knowledge. As discussed in the next chapter, your use of sources must be documented fully to avoid unintentional plagiarism.

Researching existing ideas can help you to formulate your own perspective on a subject, which will contribute to making your academic writing original. In most contexts this quality is highly valued, so enhancing the innovative nature of your work could improve your performance. However, originality is an often misunderstood term and is not as demanding as it may appear because, although your tutors expect a fresh engagement with topics from each student, they are aware of the constraints of time and experience. So, in practice and especially at undergraduate level, originality is achieved mainly through original research, which helps writers identify fresh angles on their topics.

Researching existing ideas can also give you the authority to deal with a subject effectively, because the more you know about a topic the more confident your treatment of it will be. Writers who are unclear about important issues are unlikely to organise their material well, which will have a negative impact on the quality of their writing. If you have a strong understanding of a particular topic you will be in the best position to identify the most cogent points to include or debate, which means that you will not include irrelevant data which disrupts the flow of ideas. Effective research will help you to gain clarity about the ideas and information you are discussing – this can improve your written expression to create an impression of professionalism and mastery of your material.

Keep focused on your deadline

Whilst research is usually essential to effective academic writing it is also vital to limit the time you spend locating sources so that you can maximise the time available for assessing, reading critically, and integrating sources into your assignments. The three-stage process outlined below offers tips on being efficient and effective as you gather information before you start to write. However, this is just one approach to research and you should adapt it to suit your own style as a scholar.

Collect together all the guidance you have received from your tutor about producing your piece of writing. This may include the assignment brief, the module handbook, and notes from lectures or seminars. Tutors often put coursework guidelines on the module web, so, if relevant, have a look at this. The earlier you gather these guidelines, the better your chances will be of getting support about issues you do not understand.

Here are five important questions to ask yourself when you are analysing the purpose of your writing in order to locate appropriate sources:

1 Who is the main audience for this piece of writing? (For instance, subject specialists)
2 What information should I assume this readership already knows? (I will not need to explain this in my writing)
3 What do I already know? (From lecture notes, readings, experience)
4 What background information do I need to acquire? (This should be presented in a concise way early in my writing)
5 Which key terms, concepts, or theories do I need to research? (Do I need advice about these?)

Find the right sources for your purpose

Jot down your answers to these five questions and take your notes to the library when you go to research or keep them with you as you go online to find appropriate databases via the library website. The advantage of visiting the library in person is that you may be able to speak to a library specialist on duty, who can help you to locate the best sources for your purpose.

Work with others to find suitable sources

Discuss the kinds of sources you might use with others who are studying your subject, either by chatting in person or corresponding online. Although it would be plagiarism to copy another person's work, it is good practice to search for information together, as long as you generate your own ideas for writing about the sources you find.

You could develop a joint plan for locating sources with a friend and divide the task between you; for example, if you need to investigate several theories you could research one each and report back about your findings at an agreed time, but remember to read key sources for yourself and acknowledge them in your writing. Supporting each other will make the research process more efficient and enjoyable, so collaborate with colleagues to locate information for your projects.

Begin with what you know

The aim of the lectures and other teaching sessions on your course is to prepare you for producing the written assessments, so if you have attended these regularly you should have some relevant knowledge before you begin writing an assignment. Try to take full notes when you attend any kind of class and keep these safe as a starting point for your writing projects. Begin by re-reading your notes and the handouts you received before you start to write, and jot down important points or ideas sparked by reviewing this information. Your tutors will probably provide tips about useful sources, which will be good starting points for your research.

If you find yourself in a situation where your knowledge about a topic is limited or you were unable to attend all the relevant classes, you can take some useful steps to gather together information. First, look on your module web if this is relevant and download any advice that is available about the writing you have to do. Secondly, as soon as possible contact your module tutor to make an appointment to attend at an office hour or at another suitable time. Do some preparation for this meeting, such as reading your assignment brief and making a list of questions about issues you find confusing. You could also attempt to make a plan for your writing and take this along to seek advice, or draw up a shortlist of possible sources and ask whether you have missed anything important. Thirdly, contact a classmate and ask for some tips on understanding the assignment and locating relevant sources. You could offer to help in return by reading your classmate's draft and offering constructive feedback. Or you could offer to report back on sources you locate which could be mutually useful, but be clear that you do not wish to copy or allow your classmate to copy your work.

READILY AVAILABLE SOURCES

With a little effort you can expand the range of sources which are readily available to you by using your university library's catalogue to locate a diversity of online and paper-based resources (Hacker 2006: 9).

Literature searches

Using the tips below and keeping in mind the need to be systematic, learn how to search for the literature you need for your writing. You should consult a range of different types of sources, including books, journal articles, magazines, reference works, and audiovisual sources. Although much of the source material you need is available digitally, it can be helpful to locate paper-based sources, and do not neglect the older materials and seminal works in your field because they can give you a useful grounding in your subject area.

Library catalogue

Library catalogues are gateways to a wealth of sources produced for academic audiences, and without exploiting this access to scholarly materials you cannot fulfil the central requirements of advanced level study to read widely and research independently. Although most library catalogues are intuitive to use you will benefit from attending training sessions, or reading the self-help guides available in your library and usually also downloadable from the library website.

Databases

Databases are repositories of such extensive information that they can be daunting at first, but the time you invest in learning how to use them may yield the best returns of any skill you master at university. Students who avoid databases do themselves an injustice because they shut the door on the richest selection of relevant, reliable, and readily available materials there is (Hacker 2006: 9).

Training in how to navigate around databases and use them efficiently is available at every university library, either as part of an induction programme or on request. The advantage of seeking individual training from a library specialist is that you can ask about the databases most relevant for your discipline or research project. If possible, make an appointment with a subject specialist who will give you inside information on the best places to start your search for information. As you spend time learning how to use databases you will develop your own expertise about their usefulness for different types of writing. Some databases provide access to a broad range of articles and books and these can be helpful as you begin to search, while others focus on discipline-based topics and are invaluable when you narrow down a topic for your writing.

Make sure you are equipped to work online at home by checking at your library to find out if you need a password to access databases off-campus. Whether or not you require a password to authenticate your access, you will benefit from advice about the best way to locate digital sources remotely because the route may differ from the approach you use on university computers.

Searches in catalogues and databases

Ask library specialists to advise you about the protocol for searching for sources within the databases which are most relevant for your studies (Lunsford 2008: 235). Here are some general tips, but be aware that usage can vary, so you also need to familiarise yourself with the relevant system for you:

- Attend the training sessions on using databases, search engines, and catalogues at your library
- Seek individual advice from library specialists and see the guidance on the library website
- Make notes about how to search because databases vary and it is easy to forget the individual systems
- Decide on a broad search topic to start with
- Narrow your search as soon as you can
- Be ready to discard general sources in favour of more relevant materials
- Keep notes or use a reference management system.

Although public access search engines (like Google™) are easy to use and may yield interesting general results, relying on these exclusively does not constitute scholarly practice and will severely limit the type of sources you can access. Experiment with the search engines available via your university library website and you will substantially enrich your options and access to scholarly sources (Hacker 2006: 11, Lunsford 2009: 159).

When searching:

- Decide whether to search for a key word, subject, or author depending on the options available in a database, search engine, or catalogue
- Input a key word or words for your broad search topic
- Use the advanced options to narrow your search
- Use 'and' to extend your search
- Use 'or' to distinguish between key words
- Use 'not' to refine your search
- Use double quotation marks to narrow your search like this: "academic and writing"
- Use brackets to target your search like this: (academic writing)
- Use a star to search for variations of a key word (such as write and writing) like this: write*.

Reference management systems

You can make a paper-based or a digital list of the sources you locate which appear to be appropriate for your writing. Alternatively, you can benefit from tools to help you with this time-consuming task such as RefWorks™ and EndNote™. These reference management systems are usually available via university libraries, which often provide training and support. If you are unfamiliar with these tools you should enquire at your library or ask your tutors, because once you have learnt how to use them reference management systems can save you vast amounts of time.

Special collections

Find out whether your university library has an audiovisual collection or any other specialist holdings and visit these sections to meet the specialists and familiarise yourself with the materials. You can enhance your research or writing by drawing on archives, media, or artwork which may give you a fresh angle on your topic and enable you to undertake innovative work (Lunsford 2009: 163).

Interlibrary loan and document supply

If you find out about a source that is not held in your university library and you have started to search early enough, you can take advantage of the interlibrary loan system which enables you to order material from other collections (Lunsford 2009: 163). Often you are required to complete a form that has been signed by your tutor, so find out about the protocol at your university library and plan ahead with your search for sources. Gaining access to relevant sources your library does not hold can give you an edge as a researcher and boost the quality of your work.

RELIABLE SOURCES

What constitutes reliability may vary depending on your task, but in essence you need to find the right tools for the job each time you undertake a piece of writing (Hacker 2006: 6). You also need to be assured that the content of your sources is accurate, wellfounded, and well expressed, because this will help you draw on the contents for your own work.

Digital media

Select internet sites and other digital media with care because the material may be inaccurate, incomplete, or inappropriate for academic writing (Hacker 2006: 31). Be cautious if you think the material was designed to manipulate readers or favour a particular stance. In certain cases it is useful to discuss this bias in your academic writing, but, while internet sites provide general information to get people thinking about a topic, they are not always relevant as sources for scholarly writing. You can take a number of precautions to improve the likelihood of locating useful sources online by considering the following three points.

Who is the author?

In addition to the corporate author of the website it is often possible to identify the name of a contributor or the person who wrote particular articles. This is a good sign because authors who research their material and take care to present it clearly are most likely to put their name to their work. If you can identify an author you could try using a search engine such as Google™ to check this person's affiliation, such as a university, research group, or professional organisation. This is not always important, but it is a good approach to consider who produced digital material and what the main aim might be (Hacker 2006: 25, Lunsford 2009: 171).

Are the contents attributed or acknowledged?

One sign that a website is valuable for your own writing is clear and consistent acknowledgement of sources. Although it is not always appropriate, most topics demand research and you should avoid using sites which fail to credit the material that is borrowed from elsewhere. If the authors of websites have not acknowledged their sources, you could cite material in the usual way, giving full acknowledgement to the site you have consulted, but still be accused of copying.

This is because a plagiarism detection service such as Turnitin™ can identify the unacknowledged source and may interpret the fact that you have not cited it as an intentional omission of credit. Do not think that you can solve this problem by failing to cite the website you have read because this will also be identified. So, while it can be useful to read websites before you get into more targeted research for a project, you should only borrow material from sites which follow the same scholarly codes of practice you are expected to uphold at university, because otherwise your sources could seriously let you down.

Who is the intended audience?

As you read any website you should assess the intended audience, which might be professionals in a certain field, researchers in a subject area, or scholars. Only borrow material from sites intended for scholarly use unless they happen to be relevant for your project, for example because they contain specialist information or they form part of your research topic (Lunsford 2009: 164).

Always distinguish the informal style used for writing on the internet from the academic language you are required to produce at university. Never emulate the phrasing used on websites, because even brilliant ideas will be obscured by poor written expression. This means that if you borrow ideas from internet sites it may be best to paraphrase or summarise material, so in effect you are translating material from a colloquial style into academic English.

GENERAL SOURCES

Start your research process by locating sources which provide general information about your topic. These may include:

- Dictionaries
- Encyclopaedias
- Textbooks
- Internet sites
- Newspapers
- Magazines.

The kinds of general sources you need depend upon the purpose and audience of your particular project, but every written assessment requires an initial stage of consolidating your knowledge about the topic in general (Lunsford 2009: 156). Consider which of these sources are appropriate for each piece of writing you undertake.

Dictionaries

Although the value of dictionaries is often overlooked in the initial stages of research, you might find it useful to look up key terms used in your assignment brief so that you are clear from the outset about what you are being asked to do. Your assignment brief may contain important instructions that you need to carry out in order to succeed. For example, you may be asked to **discuss** a topic, **analyse** data, or **evaluate** information. These key terms have distinctive meanings, and they imply different kinds of writing in different disciplinary contexts, so you should check with your tutor that you understand their application in your own field.

Encyclopaedias

Many people read encyclopaedias for general interest but omit to consult them for academic writing. They are useful to provide quick access to facts and fill in the basic context to boost your understanding of a general topic. Usually encyclopaedias are accessed online, but use your own judgement to assess the quality of online resources before you borrow material for your academic writing (Hacker 2006: 14).

For instance, the online source Wikipedia is used by many writers to get started on a topic, but if you choose to consult this source remember that anyone can contribute an article and consequently there is a danger that the information is inaccurate. To prevent yourself repeating errors you can check an alternative source, preferably a more scholarly one such as a textbook. If the information is corroborated you can use it for your writing, but it is often preferable to borrow information from the more scholarly source and cite that in accordance with your chosen referencing style.

Some tutors will not consider digital sources such as Wikipedia to be appropriate types of information for advanced level study owing to the lack of quality control. You can ask your tutor about this issue, but avoid using inappropriate sources you have accessed online or elsewhere because they can undermine the quality of your writing. On the other hand, the list of references accompanying the articles in Wikipedia can be very helpful in providing suggestions for general sources to consult.

Textbooks

Textbooks are particularly useful for gathering general information about a subject, and books recommended by your tutors are the best place to start. Use the contents page and the index to decide where to focus your reading so you do not waste time covering material that is not relevant for a particular assignment. Also consult the references and recommended reading lists for more targeted information on particular topics. Although textbooks provide information in an efficient way, they are designed to offer only an introduction, so you should read more advanced sources when you have become familiar with your topic in general.

Newspapers

Reading broadsheets like the *Guardian, The Times*, and the *Independent* is an excellent way to gather general information on current affairs, political debates, and economic issues, and in the course of regular reading you might come across articles about the subjects you are studying at university. Owing to the brevity of newspaper articles they are most likely to provide introductory ideas or give you a new angle on your topic, which can be a useful starting point. However, it is essential to progress to more in-depth information for your writing. You should also be aware that, except for certain assignments, tutors may not consider newspapers appropriate sources and will instead expect you to begin reading recommended readings and then conduct independent research to locate more specific information. Importantly, you should not emulate the journalistic style of newspapers, which is too informal for academic writing.

Magazines

Reading magazines like the *National Geographic* is another good way to gain awareness about general interest topics, and you may find an article dedicated to an issue you are writing about. The journalistic form and style of magazines is not usually appropriate for written assessments at university, so consider your own use of language carefully and try to locate additional, more scholarly, sources to inform your thinking and writing.

SPECIFIC SOURCES

When you have identified some general sources, the next step is to locate specific sources that will provide further insights into the subject about which you are writing. Most written assessments are set to help you gain knowledge and understanding which you can apply in new contexts; for instance, in your future career. So, you should use the process of researching and writing to demonstrate your ability to manage, synthesise, and communicate information. Specific sources may include:

- Journal articles
- Chapters in edited collections
- Chapters in monographs
- Dissertations
- Theses
- Reports.

Journal articles

There are five main reasons for locating scholarly journal articles as sources for your projects:

1 Journal articles focus on a specific topic and they engage with scholarship in that area

2 Journal articles are relatively short, so they offer a quick way to becoming familiar with a subject or debate

3 Journals are often available digitally, so you can access them easily via the databases provided on your university library website

4 Journals are usually produced four times per year, so articles allow you to access the most up-to-date research in your field

5 Journal articles are produced according to the style and format commonly used in academic disciplines, which means that not only the content but also the form is a valuable model for your own academic writing.

Although journal articles may appear to be a bit formal and technical to start with, the more you read the easier they become to understand. It is not usually necessary to read through an entire volume of a journal; instead use a database to select the articles which relate to the topic about which you are writing.

Time spent familiarising yourself with scholarly journal articles is very well invested because they provide excellent exemplars for your own writing. It is often useful to emulate the syntax, terminology, and phrasing of articles from your academic discipline to improve your written expression. Obviously you must cite any material you borrow for your writing, but it is acceptable to keep a notebook and jot down signal phrases, verbs, and terms used by scholarly authors to enhance your own vocabulary. For example, if you are simply re-using transition phrases or terms to integrate research into an argument and you are not borrowing other people's **ideas** then it may not be necessary to cite and reference. If you are unsure, you should acknowledge your source, and remember that the golden rule is that you need to credit the intellectual property of others.

Chapters in edited collections

Although you may not have time to read entire books as you move into researching specifically relevant sources, you should try to locate chapters on your topic. Often edited collections bring together specialists in a particular field, or explore themes relevant to your work. The relatively short length of chapters gives you an easy way into complex subjects, and as chapters in edited collections are self-contained they can offer a stand-alone synopsis or an interesting angle on relevant subjects. Also, the style in which chapters in edited collections are written is usually a good example of academic prose which you might want to emulate in your own writing.

Chapters in monographs

Monographs are whole books usually written by a single author based on research projects or doctoral theses. They are invaluable for providing extensive information on a specific topic and are well worth locating, not only for the content but also for the scholarly style in which they are written and the specialist language employed. However, owing to the constraints of time it is often wise to target particular chapters or to consult the index to find the most relevant passages.

Dissertations

Dissertation is the term used in the UK for research projects produced in the final year of undergraduate study or for the postgraduate degree Master of Arts, Master of Science, MPhil, and other higher qualifications. These degrees take 1 or 2 years to complete and the dissertation explores a research question in some depth.

Dissertations are usually accessible via your university library, and as they are targeted at a specific research question they can be extremely useful as a specific source for your writing. The references may be especially valuable in providing leads for your research, and as the conventions for writing dissertations vary in each subject area, may offer a model for your own work. The quality of dissertations can be variable, so you should use this resource with a particularly critical eye.

Theses

Thesis is the term used in the UK for the extended research project submitted for a PhD, DPhil, or doctorate. The length is usually equivalent to a book, and theses are sometimes revised for publication as monographs to disseminate the research in the public sphere. Many theses are not formally published but, like dissertations, they are accessible via your university library. If you identify an especially interesting thesis, it is also possible to purchase a hard copy via the British Library. You should target individual chapters or sections that are most relevant for your research by consulting the list of contents, and you should examine the references to check for sources which may prove useful for your own writing.

Reports

Reports produced by corporations, industries, organisations, government departments, research groups, and other official bodies can provide invaluable data for your own writing. Reports are often accessible online and can provide unique insights into the issues you are researching. Always apply the criteria outlined in the next section to assess the purpose and intended audience of reports so you can read them with a critical eye. Reports are usually written from a particular viewpoint, so there may be an inherent bias in the presentation of data, findings, and conclusions drawn. Like other public documents, reports are usually written with an agenda, but as long as you can identify a report's main aim and you critique the methodology you will find this kind of specific source helpful in boosting the quality of your work (Lunsford 2009: 172). The style of report writing in professional spheres may be the same as the conventions you are required to adhere to at university, but you might be required to structure your report in an alternative way and use more academic language, so check with your tutor before emulating the organisation and style of reports, especially those you access online.

SUMMARY

This chapter has stressed the value of systematic searching for sources by considering the relevance, ready availability, and reliability of materials. This focused approach to research will help you avoid wasting time because, with these criteria in mind, you are less likely to consult literature that is inappropriate or inadequate for your task.

The main arguments in this chapter:

- Get training and advice on how to use the catalogue and databases provided by your university library
- Get the right tools for the job each time you start a piece of writing by locating relevant sources
- Be prepared to reject irrelevant material at an early stage.

QUIZ

1 Why is it essential to learn how to search for sources via your university library catalogue?

2 To develop a systematic approach to searching for sources, which three Rs should you remember?

3 What is the main benefit of consulting sources which have been peer-reviewed?

4 Should you start by searching for specific or general sources first?

5 What is a monograph?

4 ASSESSING SOURCES

This chapter offers advice about effective time management by focusing on how to assess sources before spending time reading them in depth. It suggests criteria for selecting sources and reasons for rejecting material early on in your research process.

The chapter covers:

- Criteria for evaluating sources
- Selection of sources
- The intended audience of sources
- When to reject sources
- How to assess the elements within sources
- How to use sources as exemplars for your own writing.

Using this chapter

INTRODUCTION

Having looked at ways of searching systematically for literature in the previous chapter, Chapter 4 discusses how to make an initial assessment of the sources you locate. It offers criteria for evaluating sources and points out that rejecting inappropriate materials is an essential part of the research process.

CRITERIA FOR EVALUATING SOURCES

Having located both general and specific sources that you think may be relevant for your writing, you should assess the value of each text more closely before you begin reading in depth (Sopure *et al.* 1998: 410). Here is an acronym to help you remember some important criteria for evaluation:

- **Contents**
- **Relevance**
- **Interest**
- **Thesis**
- **Evidence**
- **Reliability**
- **Ingenious**
- **Author.**

Contents

Each time you undertake a piece of writing you will draw on different kinds of material, so it is difficult to specify requirements. However, you should scan the contents to focus on the areas that interest you most (Hacker 2006: 22). Try not to be distracted by irrelevant material, and if you have not found anything relevant in the contents of a source within 15 minutes you may wish to reconsider its value for your purpose.

Relevance

You need to measure the relevance of your sources against the task you have been set or the research question you have generated. Focus on the purpose of your writing and the audience you are writing for to help you decide which sources to select.

Interest

Readers tend to acquire most information and inspiration from sources in which they are interested, so if a book or article catches your eye it could be worth looking at it in more depth. If a source is interesting but not scholarly it could still be informative for your studies, but be aware that the intended audience is not academic.

Thesis

The thesis, or hypothesis, of a source is the main argument or message. If the contents are well organised it should be easy to identify the main point of a text to determine whether it is worth pursuing. If working out the main point or purpose of a source is difficult, this could be a sign that it is not suitable for your use either because it is too specialist or on account of poor argumentation on the author's part.

Evidence

If a source presents evidence to support arguments and ideas you should consider the quality of this evidence. Providing that you are aware of any limitations in the use of evidence, and that you point these out where appropriate in your own writing, you can still refer to materials with problematic use of evidence. In fact, as explored in Part 3, you should exploit your ability to identify gaps by critiquing the use of evidence as you integrate sources into your writing.

Reliability

Reliability includes accuracy, appropriate design, and authorship by people with the correct experience or expertise. Peer-reviewed sources tend to be the most reliable for academic use (Hacker 2006: 20).

Ingenious

Providing that the ideas are relevant, original perspectives on a subject can stimulate innovative ideas of your own, so if you consider a source to be ingenious in terms of its design or application it is probably worth consulting it in more detail. Notice the ways in which authors present fresh ideas and try their techniques to offer new insights in your writing where appropriate.

Author

As sources are not usually relevant unless they are authoritative, it is worth considering the background of authors to determine whether you wish to use their work. Check to see whether sources contain any information about the authors such as their affiliations, qualifications, or experience. There is often a synopsis about authors accompanying journal articles and books, and on websites you may find links to academic writers' institutions, profile pages, or published works. The more you can find out about an author, the better your sense will be of whether a source is suitable for use in your own work (Hacker 2006: 25, Lunsford 2008: 252).

Expect to reject

The danger of failing to evaluate sources effectively is that you are more likely to use inappropriate materials, which give the impression either that your research skills are inadequate, or that you are unclear about the purpose of your task. It is inevitable that you will decide to reject some materials you initially thought would be useful, and although this can be frustrating it would be more annoying to spend more time reading before realising a source is unsuitable for your purpose.

SELECTION OF SOURCES

You can assess which sources to keep and which to reject based on the following elements, although they will not all be relevant for every source:

- The title
- The subtitle
- The list of contents
- The index
- The abstract
- The subsections.

The title

If the title uses key words which reflect your own topic it may be worth checking the source more closely. However, titles can be vague or uninformative so do not rely on this information alone to assess the relevance of the source.

The subtitle if there is one

Subtitles often provide supplementary information about the focus of a source and they can be revealing when you are trying to assess the relevance. This is particularly true of journal articles because, if there is a subtitle, this often contains key words which provide hints about the focus of the source.

The list of contents if there is one

If your source contains a list of contents you can use this to navigate around the material and save yourself time by identifying individual chapters, articles, or sections that are the most worthwhile for you to read (Lunsford 2008: 258).

The index if there is one

Where edited collections and other books have an index, this is another way to save yourself time by going straight to the relevant sections. Scanning the index quickly will provide information about the contents of the source, and you can look up a key term to test the quality of the material. If the passage you are directed to is illuminating or informative, then the source is likely to be worth more of your time, but if you do not appreciate either the style or the content then you should put it aside and move on.

The abstract if there is one

Abstracts provide a synopsis of a source's scope, argument, and methodology, and they are invaluable for conveying the main points in a concise way. Abstracts often preface journal articles and they function as a kind of advertisement to inform potential readers of the main qualities and applications of an article. Reports are prefaced with an executive summary which also encapsulates the aim, findings, and methods to offer a quick means of assessing the value for your own writing.

The subsections if relevant

Glancing through a source to identify the main components can throw light on the usefulness for your purpose. For journal articles, book chapters, and other material that is subdivided you can choose which parts to focus on, but always skim read the rest because otherwise you could miss important points or misunderstand the argument all together. You could hone in on the introduction and conclusion to gain an idea about the contents before deciding where to focus your attention.

THE INTENDED AUDIENCE OF SOURCES

In addition to assessing the contents of potentially useful sources, you need to analyse other qualities before you spend time reading them in detail. In particular, you should reflect on the intended audience to identify whether sources are sufficiently formal for use in your academic writing.

Unless you are researching a topic that requires you to consult other types of materials, you should concentrate on gathering scholarly sources aimed at academic or specialist readerships. The benefit of using scholarly sources is that the authors are more likely to have observed the code of scholarly practice you need to adhere to as an academic writer. For instance, scholarly sources tend to be based on research or first-hand information and they acknowledge borrowed material through accurate citation and referencing.

To help you analyse whether a source is suitable for your audience you can ask yourself these four questions:

1 Is the language formal, specialist, or technical?
2 Is the source well organised?
3 Is the source clearly expressed?
4 Is the content comprehensive?

Language

If the language in which a source is written is colloquial, journalistic, or informal, it may still be valuable, but you need to ensure that your own writing remains academic in style and content unless your task demands a different form of expression. It is especially useful to read sources which use specialist language because this helps you become fluent in the jargon of your discipline.

Organisation

The format and organising principles of a source provide clues about the intended audience and, although scholarly sources are complex, they are usually well planned. As you are selecting sources also notice how the information is organised to gain hints about ways you can order your own thoughts in your academic writing.

Written expression

If a source is not well written it might still be interesting for your research, but avoid wasting time trying to identify the main points if they are not well articulated. Material that has been poorly presented is confusing, so if you get the impression that the execution of a document is faulty you should move on to consult more scholarly material.

Comprehensive accounts

Sources which deal only superficially with a subject can also be misleading so you may wish to choose in-depth analyses and comprehensive accounts to extend your knowledge and understanding. This does not mean that you need to read entire sources but, as suggested above, you can use the list of contents, the index, or the subsections to navigate around the material and scan less relevant parts to concentrate your time and attention on the most important elements (Hacker 2006: 22).

SUMMARY

This chapter has focused on how to assess sources before spending time reading them in depth. It has presented criteria for selecting sources and reasons for rejecting material early in your research process. The next chapter builds upon this discussion by looking at how to read sources critically.

The main arguments in this chapter:

- Researchers need criteria for evaluating sources
- You should apply these criteria early in the research process to avoid wasting time
- Every writing task requires different types of sources.

QUIZ

1 In the acronym CRITERIA used above to outline how to evaluate sources, what does the letter 'T' stand for?

2 If you notice limitations with the use of evidence in a source, how can you turn this to your advantage?

3 Will you need to reject some of the sources you locate using your university's library catalogue?

4 Why is it useful to look at the index of a source?

5 What is an abstract?

5 ▷ READING SOURCES CRITICALLY

This chapter explores how to interrogate the use of evidence in the sources you read and refer to in your writing. It discusses how to assess authors' credentials and identify limitations in the literature related to your topic. It also considers a range of reading strategies, including skimming and scanning.

The chapter covers:

- Keeping complete records
- Critiquing authors' credentials
- Critiquing the reliability of sources
- Skimming
- Scanning
- Planning
- Primary evidence
- Secondary evidence
- Bias.

Using this chapter

INTRODUCTION

Having stressed the need to make an initial assessment of how useful sources might be for your purpose in the previous chapter, Chapter 5 extends this topic to look in more depth at critical reading as part of the research process and a prelude to effective academic writing.

COMPLETE RECORDS

As you read potential sources for your academic writing, remember that you will need a complete set of records when you document these sources in your writing. You should identify the author and date for each source, and if you find particularly relevant material you should make a note of the page numbers. When reading **books**, jot down the following:

- The authors' full names
- The date
- The chapter title if relevant
- The book title
- The place where the book was published
- The publisher
- The page numbers if you borrow data from a specific page
- The web address if you accessed the book online
- The date of access if you accessed the book online.

When reading **journal articles** jot down the following:

- The authors' full names
- The date
- The article title
- The journal
- The volume
- The part or issue number, if there is one
- The page numbers if you borrow data from a specific page
- The web address if you accessed the journal online
- The date of access if you accessed the journal online.

When reading **websites** jot down the following:

- The corporate author
- The date
- The webpage title

- The web address
- The date of access.

Although you will consult a range of other types of sources, as shown in Chapter 10, these are usually referenced as variations of books, journal articles, and websites. **Before you start to read sources you should familiarise yourself with the referencing style that is recommended in your subject area so that you know which information to record as you are making notes.**

CRITICAL READING

Critical reading is a vital component of successful academic writing, because if you integrate sources into your work without a full understanding of their contents and relative merits for your purpose, you can undermine your academic success (Lunsford 2009: 17). One way to identify the qualities of your sources is to share ideas with colleagues and friends. Copying another writer's ideas is plagiarism, and collusion (which means co-writing an assignment that you submit as your own work) is also a form of plagiarism that is penalised at university. However, unless your tutor advises you otherwise, it is expected that you will debate the sources you read and the topics you are studying both in class and less formally in your own time to form your own perspective on the issues.

Skimming

Skimming means observing the surface features of a source to identify the main components (Lunsford 2008: 28). This is useful when you first start to read a text because it enables you to map out the contents to assess their value for your purpose. As you are scanning a source you should make a note of the title, key words, and section headings as well as gaining a sense of the contents, including any graphics, statistics, lists, or other elements which may be important for your writing. Here is a list of the areas to observe as you skim read a source:

- Title
- Subtitle if relevant
- Key words if listed
- Headings
- Subheadings
- Graphics
- Statistics
- Figures
- Tables.

As you skim a text it can be useful to read the first sentence of each paragraph because, if a text is well written, you can trace the line of argument quickly in this way. When you see this done effectively you will appreciate how accessible it makes the information and you may wish to adopt this approach to setting out main points in your own writing.

Scanning

Scanning means using the information you have gleaned through skimming to focus on the parts of the text that are most valuable to you. Critical reading places an emphasis on evaluating the contents, so keep your topics or research question firmly in mind to select the passages that are of greatest relevance to this. If your source has a separate introduction you should scan this element to establish the scope and focus. If there is a conclusion you should scan this to understand the implications of the discussion. To help you identify which sections to scan in more detail, here is a list of possible foci:

- Reflect on the purpose of your own writing
- Generate a question or focus for your reading
- Read the source quickly until you come to a potentially useful section or point
- Read this section in detail and jot down the information it provides
- Record the details you need to cite and reference, including page numbers
- Make a note of your thoughts about this passage for your writing
- Jot down any criticisms you have about the content or style of this passage.

Planning

The purpose of skimming and scanning a text is to plan for your own writing, so your observations should feed into your plans for a specific project or assignment. It is easy to spend too much time researching and lose sight of your writing goal, so each time you undertake critical reading make full notes and orientate them towards a section of your work-in-progress.

It can be useful to intersperse critical reading with drafting to build up your argument gradually based on the information contained in sources and the ideas they generate for your own work. Discover the approach that works best for you, but keep an eye on your deadline and avoid spending more time than necessary reading without writing because you may go off track and waste time on material you will not need.

BE CRITICAL ABOUT AUTHORS' CREDENTIALS

As you read each source you may gain an overall feeling about whether you believe the author's argument or trust the approach that has been adopted. You can develop more of a sense of an author's credentials by analysing the style, content, and organisation of a source.

Style

You may question an author's credentials if the style in which a source is presented is informal or unprofessional. Although informality is appropriate in some contexts, it is not conventional in academia so a lack of formality can signal that an author is not aiming for a scholarly audience, which means that the source might not have the right credentials for you to use it in your academic writing.

If the language is emotive this may be a sign that an author is too involved in the subject matter to present a balanced argument. You might find this perspective useful for your purpose and, depending on your project, you may choose to critique the tone in your writing. However, in some cases using such texts could detract from the professionalism of your own work, so ask yourself whether it would be preferable to seek out more scholarly sources.

Poor presentation might include badly edited text or a lack of document integrity, which means that the elements within a source are out of order – for example, the numbering of sections could be inaccurate. You should be particularly wary if a source has not been proofread properly because this can be a sign that authors have not been professional in writing and revising their material. If these obvious types of errors exist there may be more substantial problems in the design and articulation of information, which could render the source problematic for your use.

Content

You would be likely to question an author's credentials if a source only covered a subject partially or offered information you knew to be inaccurate (Lunsford 2009: 171). The most relevant material for academic use introduces the scope and focus clearly out of respect for readers, and in accordance with scholarly practice. As you will need to read a variety of topics it would be difficult to provide a list of all the features to look out for, but you should aim to generate a mental list of the kinds of content you require for each writing task, which could include the following:

- What assumptions does the author make?
- How detailed is the source?

Organisation

Poorly organised texts can be problematic for academic use, so as you are reading be prepared to reject badly planned materials. On the other hand, well-planned sources provide potential exemplars for your own writing when the contents are clearly set out. Notice how your sources are ordered, in particular how authors introduce their arguments by hooking the reader's attention with innovative approaches and interest-grabbing ideas.

Reading with a critical eye is essential to developing your own aptitude for ordering material, so reflect upon the organisation of the main body of academic texts to identify how the material has been subdivided. In some disciplines the use of subheadings is conventional, whereas in other subjects writers move between paragraphs using transition phrases to mark developments in the argument. Focus on the concluding section of well organised texts to identify techniques you might try for bringing the discussion to a close with impact and style.

CRITIQUING THE RELIABILITY OF SOURCES

The reliability of source material is a concern throughout the research process but especially when you are reading critically because you have the opportunity to analyse this crucial issue in more depth (Lunsford 2008: 28). You need to evaluate the assumptions made by authors and the subjectivity of their arguments and, although the focus of your critical reading will depend on your main purpose, each time you tackle a piece of writing there are seven questions you can use to prompt your analysis:

1 Does the source use primary evidence?

2 Does the source use secondary evidence?

3 Is the evidence convincing?

4 What are the author's credentials?

5 What assumptions does the author make?

6 What subjectivity or bias is evident in the source?

7 Is the language emotive?

Evidence

Not all sources draw upon evidence so this issue is not a concern every time you are reading, but if use of evidence is a feature you should evaluate this as an indicator of the source's reliability. You can start by checking whether the evidence is integrated professionally and acknowledged using appropriate citation and referencing. Then look at the date of the evidence to see whether it is current, or if there is a good reason for using older material – for instance, this can be appropriate when citing seminal works or influential ideas from the past (Lunsford 2009: 171). Next, consult the references in more detail to see whether the evidence is primary or secondary.

Does the source use primary evidence?

Primary evidence has a distinctive meaning in different disciplinary contexts, so make sure you clarify the meaning in your field by asking your tutor or other subject specialists if you are unsure. In most contexts primary evidence refers to data that is directly related to the topic being discussed; this may include research findings, interviews, recordings, images, objects, and other documents giving direct information about a subject – for example, a diary provides primary evidence about a person's life. Primary evidence has a particular meaning in the legal context where it is known as primary authority for the law, which includes cases, acts, directives, treatises, and legislation (Foster 2009: 57).

Use of primary evidence in the sources you read can establish authority by demonstrating authors' first-hand familiarity with subjects. Nevertheless, if a book or article uses primary evidence you should analyse the authenticity by checking whether the acknowledgements are systematic, clear, and complete. If the text you are reading uses badly presented primary data, do not rely on this information but instead try to find alternative materials with more scholarly use of sources. You may also wish to critique the use of evidence in the source if that is suitable for your written work.

Does the source use secondary evidence?

Secondary evidence can have a specific meaning in different disciplines so you should check the usage in your own field. In most contexts secondary evidence refers to information *about* a subject such as interpretations, theories, and explanations. In the legal context secondary evidence is known as secondary authority for the law, which includes an account, commentary, or a criticism of the law (Foster 2009: 58).

Texts as secondary evidence

Most books and journal articles constitute secondary evidence because they discuss and analyse the subjects you are studying, although they may also contain primary evidence. The benefit of reading other people's interpretations is that you can gain ideas to develop your own perspectives, but as you read you should consider the reliability of the interpretation and jot down both strengths and weaknesses which you can write about as appropriate. If your own writing demands critical thinking, make sure you undertake analysis as you integrate material into your work. This is discussed in Chapter 9, which concentrates on critiquing sources.

Texts that analyse secondary evidence

Many books and journal articles refer to existing literature and analyse the arguments advanced by other scholars. As you read you should reflect upon the quality of this analysis and be prepared to identify any weaknesses in the evaluation of other sources if that is required.

Although at first you may not feel confident about critiquing an author's treatment of other works, criticality is a core feature of successful academic writing. Critiquing has a distinctive meaning in academia and it requires a balanced approach that identifies both strengths and weaknesses in the material you are discussing. Reading reviews of books and articles as well as texts containing analyses of other people's ideas is an excellent way to strengthen your own ability to critique. Try making a note of the types of points other people make and eventually you will have a framework in your own mind for the kinds of comments you could make.

Here is a list of some issues you might identify as you are critiquing an author's use of other sources:

- Little or no analysis of any secondary sources to which the author refers
- Weak analysis of any secondary sources to which the author refers
- Poor attribution of secondary sources
- A limitation in the type, topic, or scope of secondary sources to which the author refers.

With practice you will find it easier to pick out problems in authors' use of sources and it will become increasingly obvious when the content is unreliable or incomplete. The more you test your skills of critiquing by writing in an analytical way, the stronger your own style of evaluating sources will become.

Is the evidence convincing?

Related to the reliability of the sources you read, another important issue to consider is how convincing the use of evidence is in your view. This issue is applicable to use of both primary and secondary evidence, and the following four questions regarding gaps in the use of evidence are designed to prompt your reflection as you are reading:

1 Are there disjunctions between the points made and the supporting evidence given?
2 Is there a lack of up-to-date evidence?
3 Is there a bias in the information or ideas presented?
4 Is there inadequate citation or referencing?

Disjunction between points made and supporting evidence

One issue that can undermine the reliability of a source is a lack of congruity between an author's argument and the information provided to back this up. To analyse this in a source you are reading you can try the exercise in the box on p. 63.

In this way you can turn flaws in your sources into opportunities to show your acumen as a scholar by discussing problematic use of evidence which undermines the reliability of the argument.

A lack of up-to-date evidence

As mentioned above, there are occasions when authors cite texts dating back to an earlier decade or century, especially if they are referring to primary evidence. When

Analysing supporting evidence

- Select a source to analyse
- Record all the details you need to cite and reference this source, including the page numbers as appropriate
- Select a paragraph in the main body of this source that contains evidence of some kind
- Jot down the point the author makes in this paragraph
- Then examine the evidence to determine how well it supports this point
- Make a note of any gaps you observe between the author's argument and the supporting evidence.

discussing secondary sources it can also be appropriate to acknowledge influential figures from the past who have had an impact on scholarly debate. However, if you are reading a source published relatively recently which contains few up-to-date citations, this may be an indication that the author has not researched the topic thoroughly. Depending on the purpose of your own writing it may be valuable to point out this limitation as you refer to the source. Use this as a reminder that, whenever possible, you should try to discuss current sources in your own writing to demonstrate your effectiveness as a researcher and your ability to engage fully with the subject matter.

Bias in the information or ideas presented

All writing contains bias, which means that it displays sympathy with a particular theory, viewpoint, or interpretation of the topic you are studying. Successful scholars compensate for an inherent propensity to bias by exploring counterarguments and contrasting perspectives in their arguments. So sources which present multiple perspectives are usually the most reliable for your studies. On the other hand, texts which contain bias offer you a chance to demonstrate your critical thinking by pointing out opposing views which have not been considered or highlighting the prejudice an author displays.

Be aware that your own writing naturally contains bias and when it is appropriate try to balance the perspective you are drawn to initially with careful consideration of other angles. Reading well balanced arguments will help you develop this valuable ability to address counterclaims, so as you are reading take note of the ways in which successful scholars produce well rounded debates.

Inadequate citation or referencing

The failure to acknowledge influences is a serious flaw that undermines the reliability of the sources you read. Unless referencing is not conventional in the type of text you are reading, for instance because it is non-academic, you should expect to see clear acknowledgements of the data and ideas the authors have drawn on in their work. As scholarship is founded upon recognition of other people's contributions to knowledge, you may not consider it useful to consult a source that does not adopt this scholarly practice. If you do choose to use poorly referenced materials for your own writing, ask yourself whether it is appropriate to comment on this limitation; it will not always be necessary but it is vital that you notice this as you are reading.

SUMMARY

This chapter has recommended that you take note of whether authors analyse the evidence they draw upon and has suggested that you should be prepared to point out the limitations you have spotted. In conjunction with Chapter 3, which is about locating sources, and Chapter 4, which is about assessing sources, this chapter has provided tips on reading sources critically by looking for gaps in the use of evidence, failure to cite and reference, or excessive bias.

Together, the chapters in Part 2 introduce a research strategy called LARC, which stands for Locate, Assess, and Read Critically. This is an approach you can adopt and adapt as appropriate as you prepare to write assessments at an advanced level. Having undertaken some research and reading, the next step is writing, which is tackled in Part 3 with a focus on different techniques for integrating sources into your work.

The main arguments in this chapter:

- Always read with a critical eye
- Take notes as you read about the content and style of sources
- Jot down the limitations you spot
- Record all the information you need to cite and reference sources, including page numbers.

QUIZ

The extract below is from an article by Ng and Feldman called 'Personality, Social Relationships, and Vocational Indecision Among College Students: The Meditating Effects of Identity Construction' (2009). Read the extract and then answer the questions to test your critical reading.

> ### A role identity perspective on vocational indecision
>
> According to role identity theory (Stryker 1980, Tajfel and Turner 1985), individuals possess as many identities as they occupy positions (or roles) in networks of social relationships. Each role involves a set of social expectations. Role

➡

identities, then, can be conceptualized as internalized role expectations that define the self-concept (Katz and Kahn 1978, Stryker and Burke 2000). Individuals' self-concepts are made up of the meanings they attach to the multiple roles they play in the society. While individuals have multiple role identities, though, some role identities are more salient than others. These salient role identities have the greatest meaning to a person and therefore contribute the most to his/her definition of self-concept (Hogg 2000).

Salient role identities play several important functions in individuals' lives. First, the most salient identities provide overarching schemas through which individuals interpret and respond to life events (Vignoles et al. 2006). Second, these identities provide individuals with a sense of direction for their lives and guide their behaviours when they are faced with novel or uncertain situations (Reitz and Murtan 1994, Suh 2002). Third, when individuals change from one life stage to another, the salient life roles they have to play are likely to change as well (Super 1980). For many college students and graduates, the two most salient life roles are student and worker (Super 1990). These two identities, therefore, will be the focus of the current study.

(Ng and Feldman 2009: 312)

1 What is the main topic of this extract?

2 In the first paragraph of the extract above, how many citations do Ng and Feldman give for role identity theory and from which decade do they date?

3 According to Ng and Feldman, which identities have the greatest meaning to a person? (Salient role identities or other kinds?)

4 Ng and Feldman argue that for many students the two most salient life roles are student and worker, and they cite Super to support this point. What is the date of this source?

5 Which two identities does this article by Ng and Feldman focus on?

PART 3

WRITING

INTRODUCTION TO PART 3

Part 3 shows how you can integrate sources into your writing by using the techniques of quoting, paraphrasing, summarising, and critiquing. It also explains that when using these methods you must demonstrate academic integrity by citing the authors and providing page numbers where appropriate. While these techniques for integrating sources into your writing are discussed in separate chapters, you should try to use each of them as you refer to existing research in your writing. This will ensure a balanced approach to using the literature in your field and indicate your control over the sources you have selected for analysis.

Chapter 6 defines quoting and demonstrates how to cite quotations. Chapter 7 defines paraphrasing and shows how to acknowledge paraphrase extracts from sources. Chapter 8 defines the two main types of summarising and discusses how to integrate summaries into your writing. Building on these three techniques, Chapter 9 defines critiquing and emphasises the need to evaluate source material as you weave it into your own work.

Before reading Part 3, you should remember that all writers are indebted to existing knowledge (Howard 2007: 13) and that acknowledging scholars is a fundamental requirement of academic writing. If you omit citations as you integrate other people's ideas into your writing, you will be breaking the code of scholarly practice by plagiarising.

Do not resist the requirement to acknowledge your sources, because by citing you fulfil marking criteria and demonstrate your ability to conduct research (Neville 2007: 12). Crucially, distinguishing between existing literature and your own ideas is the main way you can contribute to knowledge by building upon and critiquing what others have written (Howard 2007: 13).

Part 3 is designed to help you distinguish between existing research and your own ideas, and boost your confidence as a writer. The main message of the following four chapters is that as you integrate sources into your writing you must cite appropriately to avoid plagiarism. Remember:

1 Integrate quotes only when there is a good reason to do so
2 Integrate paraphrases with accuracy
3 Integrate summaries to cover lots of information efficiently
4 Aim to *critique* when you borrow material from sources.

INTEGRATING SOURCES BY QUOTING

This chapter explains how to quote and cite sources in your academic writing. It discusses how to introduce and integrate quotes into your writing and how to analyse sources as appropriate.

The chapter covers:

- Quoting sources
- Acknowledging sources, including the page numbers
- In-text citations
- Quoting short extracts
- Quoting long extracts
- Use of punctuation when quoting.

Using this chapter

INTRODUCTION

Having introduced the LARC research strategy in Part 2, Chapter 6 explains how to integrate literature into your writing by quoting. It focuses on the need to acknowledge authors by citing, and emphasises that page numbers must be given each time you quote.

QUOTING

The word 'quote' is short for quotation, which means to repeat exactly the words used by a writer or speaker within quotation marks. You can use double or single quotation marks depending on the guidelines in your chosen referencing style, and whichever you use you should check you have been consistent throughout your document.

Acknowledging your sources

When you are quoting you must give an in-text citation stating the author's surname and the date of the source (Lunsford 2008: 262). You should also give the page number so readers can locate the exact passage. In addition to this in-text citation, you must give the full publication details in your list of references at the end of your work in accordance with your chosen referencing style. Below is an example of quoting with an in-text citation in the Harvard style. This passage quotes ideas from an article by Gornall called 'Whistleblowing: The Price of Silence' (2009).

> In his recent article 'Whistleblowing: The Price of Silence', Gornall argues that 'despite the repeated assurances of politicians', whistleblowers in the National Health Service are still 'an endangered species' (2009: 1000).

Here is an example of the accompanying entry in the list of references at the end of the writing:

> Gornall, J. (2009) Whistleblowing: The Price of Silence. *British Medical Journal* **339**: 1000–4.

Why quote sources?

Quotes can be useful if a writer or speaker has articulated an idea with particular clarity and you want to capture the exact phrasing. Quoting can be helpful when you wish to give an authoritative definition from a scholarly source, and quotes are essential if you wish to reproduce the precise words used by another person, for instance when you are analysing a literary or historical text.

Although quoting can show readers you have researched a topic, you should use quotes with **caution** because stating word-for-word what someone else has said or written does not demonstrate your own understanding of the text. So quote sparingly and avoid simply cutting and pasting text into your own writing. Balance quoting with paraphrasing and summarising, and remember to combine quotes with evidence of your own critical thinking (Williams and Carroll 2009: 30).

A common reason for integrating sources into an essay by quoting is to provide evidence for an argument. So when you are searching for and selecting possible quotes, remember to focus on what you wish to argue, and choose material that either backs up your position or demonstrates alternative perspectives. It might be useful to try jotting down your ideas before you search for sources because this can help you to be more discerning in the kind of information you seek, although it is vital to keep an open mind as you are reading. Tutors often supply reading lists, which you should consult when you tackle the related assignments.

HOW TO QUOTE SHORT EXTRACTS

Before you quote from a source you should make sure that the source is appropriate for your piece of writing. Badly chosen material can interrupt the flow of your argument or the logic of your document and undermine the overall quality of your work. As you are planning an essay, report, critique, analysis, or other type of written assessment, identify where it would be most effective to integrate quotes and keep this under review as you are drafting.

Quotes should always be integrated with a clear introduction to the source and a comment about the value in relation to the argument you are making. If you throw sources into your writing with no analysis or interpretation you will not gain much credit from markers, but if you explain what is pertinent and critique the source you will gain credit for selecting, assessing, and applying sources for your purpose as appropriate. When appropriate, discuss the implications of what others have argued and build upon existing knowledge to develop your own ideas.

Here are some examples of how you can quote from sources to develop your own argument. Read the extract below by Howard from her article 'Understanding "internet plagiarism"' (2007). Note the features identified by the arrows.

Howard points out that all writers are indebted to their predecessors, and she discusses two sources in relation to this point; one source is by Rose (1993) and the other is by Porter (1986).

> ## Understanding 'internet plagiarism'
>
> Copyright historian Mark Rose has gone so far as to say that cultural production, including textual production, 'is always a matter of appropriation and transformation' (1993, p. 135). James Porter brought the issue to composition and rhetoric, asserting that writers work from their own 'unaccountable collections of incompatible ideas, beliefs, and sources' (1986, p. 35). Thus, from an intertextual point of view, all writers are always collaborating with text.
>
> (Howard 2007: 9)

The author summarises Rose's argument, quoting and citing with page numbers

The author identifies Porter's contribution to the debate, quoting and citing his argument

Importantly, the author then states her own argument which builds upon the earlier sources

Notice that Howard does not simply record what others have written – she also puts forward her own argument which is indebted to the authors she cites but clearly differentiated from their intellectual property. Howard uses a variation of the Harvard style that requires her to format the date and page slightly differently to the method used in this book. For more information about variations of the Harvard style, see Chapter 10.

In your own writing you can use this technique of drawing upon existing literature to build up evidence in support of the argument you are making. Before drafting your ideas you should jot down the sources you wish to use and identify which points you want to build upon in particular. Make sure that you record the information needed for your in-text citations, including the page numbers as Howard has done here, and make a note of the full publication details for your list of references.

SYNTHESISING QUOTES INTO YOUR OWN ARGUMENT

Always introduce your source and comment after quoting to relate it to the argument you are making. Here is an example of how you might synthesise material from Howard's article (2007) into your writing:

> Howard argues that internet plagiarism is misunderstood, and she suggests that academics should 'gain a more tempered, critical understanding' of this issue (2007: 4). Although Howard is correct in this assessment, this is a particularly complex challenge within contemporary higher education.

In this example the writer mentions the author of the source within her sentence and then gives the date and page number within an in-text citation in brackets. When you do not mention authors' names in your own writing you should give the surname within your in-text citations.

Notice that in this example the writer mentions Howard to signal the use of this · source and distinguish it from her own ideas. The writer summarises a point made by Howard, then quotes the source, giving the date and page number. After this the writer comments on the source, which demonstrates the ability to analyse texts and relate them to her own discussion. Try to follow this pattern in your own writing:

- **Signal your use of sources and introduce them clearly**
- **Summarise the author's argument and quote if appropriate**
- **Synthesise the source into your own writing by analysing or interpreting the ideas.**

By adopting this three-step approach to synthesising sources in your writing you can boost the criticality of your work. Tutors usually expect you to process the information you draw upon and bring together ideas in a way which adds value to them by revealing new insights and applications. In this way you can contribute to the work of academics by constructing knowledge based upon existing work mixed with analysis and your own unique perspective.

MAKING CHANGES TO MATERIAL YOU QUOTE

It is usually best to quote exactly what an author has written or a person has said, but sometimes you will need to make text grammatically correct within your own writing, and on other occasions you might wish to clarify or specify a point. If you change any element within the material you quote, you should indicate the change using square brackets (Lunsford 2009: 344). Here is an example:

> We should reconsider the role of the internet in 'our [academic] culture of authorship' (Howard 2007: 4).

If you add or remove capital letters you should also put the text you have changed into square brackets. Check the guidelines in your chosen referencing style for further information and follow the instructions with care.

Use of ellipses

If you wish to omit part of a quote you should use an ellipsis, which means inserting three full points to signal the missing text (Lunsford 2009: 344). Here is an example:

> Therefore, the history of textual production 'reveals that previous revolutions in access to text . . . also incited cultural fears' (Howard 2007: 4).

You should not normally begin or end a quote with an ellipsis because readers are aware that there was text before and after the extract you have borrowed. However, check your chosen referencing style for guidance.

Use of italics

It is not normally necessary to italicise quotes, and you should not do so unless you are directed to do so by your tutor or you know that this is the accepted practice in your discipline. Consult the instructions in your chosen referencing style on this matter. If you do choose to italicise quotes, make sure that you use quotation marks so that it is clear which words are your own and which words come from a source. Check you have introduced and commented upon the sources you quote.

Avoid using quotation marks when you are not quoting

You must use quotation marks whenever you quote a source word-for-word, but you should avoid using quotation marks for other purposes such as emphasis or irony (Lunsford 2009: 344). It is advisable to avoid using quotation marks when you are not reporting the words of others because this can be disruptive for readers. Here is an example of disruptive and unnecessary quotation marks:

> The Director of the company referred to the take-over bid as a 'cat fight' (Higgins 2010: 3).

Where does the punctuation go?

Notice that in the example above, the full stop comes at the end of the sentence after the in-text citation. You should observe the usual practice in the scholarly sources recommended by your tutors, and remember that the appropriate punctuation for quotes depends on the context and the specific guidelines in your chosen referencing style. If you use a numerical referencing system, for instance, the full stop goes at the end of the sentence before the superscript number, like this.[1]

HOW TO QUOTE LONG EXTRACTS

If you are quoting more than approximately 20 words you can separate the quote from your own writing and indent it. You should not use quotation marks when you indent quotes because this formatting tells readers that you have borrowed the material from a source (Williams and Carroll 2009: 32).

[1] This is an example of where to punctuate when using a numerical referencing style.

The same rules for integrating material into your own writing apply as when you quote shorter passages, so remember to signal your use of a source with a clear introduction, summarise or quote as appropriate, and synthesise the ideas into your own work by interpreting or analysing the material. An example is shown in the box below.

According to Howard (2007), academics should reflect upon historical cultural developments to understand the impact of the internet for student writers today. She argues that the history of text:

[R]eveals that previous revolutions in access to text, such as those precipitated by the advent of the printing press and again by mass education, also incited cultural fears. This time, the cultural fears are focused on issues of property and especially on students' incursions on the words and ideas of others. If, however, we consider not just access to text but also textual relationships, we can gain a more tempered, critical understanding of Internet plagiarism.

(Howard 2007: 4)

Based on Howard's argument, the author interviewed 30 academics from the School of Art and invited them to suggest ways of helping student writers analyse the interplay between their writing and material from the internet. The findings are presented in the following chapter.

In the example above, the writer uses Howard's argument as a springboard into her own enquiry about internet plagiarism. Notice that this writer draws upon Howard's point to inform her own research and she acknowledges this source fully. The writer could have paraphrased or summarised Howard's argument, but she chose to quote from the source because she wanted to capture the exact words. This writer's use of this source may have been more effective if she had paraphrased the material, and you can see how she might have done that in the next chapter.

SUMMARY

This chapter has given the rationale for quoting and explained how to quote and acknowledge your sources using in-text citations. It has pointed out that quotes must be introduced and integrated into your writing with comments as appropriate.

The main arguments in this chapter:

- Choose quotations with care
- Vary quoting with paraphrasing and summarising
- Acknowledge the sources you quote, including the page numbers.

QUIZ

The extract below is from an article by Moore et al. called 'Explaining the Rise in Antidepressant Prescribing: A Descriptive Study Using the General Practice Research Database' (2009). Read the extract and then answer the questions to test your knowledge about accurate quoting and citation.

Conclusions

Antidepressant prescribing is much higher compared with 10 years ago. This increase is not because of an increase in the incidence of new cases of depression, a lower threshold for treatment, an increase in the proportion of new cases of depression for whom antidepressants are prescribed, or an increase in the duration of the prescriptions written for new cases of depression. Rather, the dramatic changes in antidepressant prescribing volumes between 1993 and 2005 seem to be largely because more patients are on long term medication and this group consumes the most drugs. In order to better understand the rise in antidepressant prescribing, research needs to focus on chronic prescribing and policy needs to focus on encouraging appropriate high quality monitoring and review of those patients who become established on long term prescriptions.

(Moore et al. 2009: 7)

---

1 Is this quotation and citation accurate?

Example 1

The recent study by Moore et al. reveals that 'Antidepressant prescribing is much higher compared with 10 years ago' (2009: 7).

---

2 Is this quotation and citation accurate?

Example 2

Moore et al. argue that this 'increase is not because of an increase in the incidence of new cases of depression, a lower threshold for treatment, an increase in the proportion of new cases of depression for whom antidepressants are prescribed, or an increase in the duration of the prescriptions written for new cases of depression' (2009: 7). This is a powerful argument and the topic is timely.

---

3 Is this quotation and citation accurate?

Example 3

According to Moore et al. 'dramatic changes in antidepressant prescribing volumes between 1993 and 2005' seem to be largely because more patients are on long term medication and this group consumes the most drugs (2009: 7). This finding has implications for the economics of patient care.

---

4 Is this quotation and citation accurate?

Example 4

Moore et al. conclude that *to better understand the rise in antidepressant prescribing, research needs to focus on chronic prescribing and policy needs* (2009). Their call for further research is relevant to practitioners across the UK.

---

5 Is this quotation and citation accurate?

Example 5

'In order to better understand the rise in antidepressant prescribing, research needs to focus on chronic prescribing and policy needs to focus on encouraging appropriate high quality monitoring and review of those patients who become established on long term prescriptions' (Moore et al. 2009: 7).

---

7 ▶ INTEGRATING SOURCES BY PARAPHRASING

This chapter explains how to paraphrase and cite sources in your academic writing. It discusses how to introduce and integrate paraphrases into your writing and how to analyse sources as appropriate.

The chapter covers:

■ Paraphrasing sources

■ Acknowledging sources, usually including the page numbers

■ In-text citations

■ Understanding sources

■ Selecting extracts to paraphrase

■ Use of punctuation when paraphrasing.

Using this chapter

INTRODUCTION

Having explained how to quote in the previous chapter, Chapter 7 shows how you can integrate sources into your own writing by paraphrasing. It focuses on the need to acknowledge authors by citing and emphasises that page numbers must be given each time you paraphrase. However, check your referencing guidelines for instructions as practice can vary.

PARAPHRASING

To paraphrase a source means to put it into your own words in an accurate way, so be careful not to distort the meaning as you rephrase the words. A paraphrase of a source should be approximately the same length as the original passage (Neville 2007: 36).

Acknowledging your sources

When you paraphrase you must give an in-text citation stating the author's surname and the date of the source. You should usually give the page number so readers can locate the exact passage; check this with your tutor if you are unsure. In addition to this in-text citation you must give the full publication details in your list of references in accordance with your chosen referencing style. Below is an example of a paraphrase with an in-text citation in the Harvard style. This passage paraphrases ideas from an article by Gornall called 'Whistleblowing: The Price of Silence' (2009).

> In his recent article 'Whistleblowing: The Price of Silence' Gornall argues that, although politicians have promised things will change, there are very few people who criticise errors in the National Health Service (2009: 1000).

Here is an example of the accompanying entry in the list of references at the end of the writing:

> Gornall, J. (2009) Whistleblowing: The Price of Silence. *British Medical Journal* **339**: 1000–4.

Why paraphrase sources?

Paraphrasing is a useful means of demonstrating your understanding of a text, and in many instances this technique for integrating sources into your writing is more appropriate than quoting because it reveals your insight into the issues you are discussing. Remember to combine paraphrasing with evidence of your own critical thinking by analysing sources as you integrate them. Try to summarise some sources (see Chapter 8) as well as paraphrasing because this allows you to convey lots of information in a concise manner.

HOW TO PARAPHRASE

Before you paraphrase an extract from a source you should make sure the text is appropriate for your piece of writing. Badly chosen passages can interrupt the flow of your argument or the logic of your document and thus undermine the overall quality of your work. Aim to identify the strengths and weaknesses of sources so you use them in an analytical mode rather than taking the contents at face value.

As you analyse potentially useful sources consider whether they provide reliable support for the points you are making or whether they add value to your writing, for instance by showing an alternative perspective. When appropriate, aim to discuss the implications of what others have argued for your own argument to build upon existing knowledge and develop your own critical thinking.

Discuss sources with others

As you are planning to draft your ideas, identify where it would be most effective to integrate paraphrased material and keep this under review as you are drafting. When you are certain that a source is useful for your purpose and will enhance rather than detract from your own writing, check that you fully understand the argument that is being made. If your friends have read the same source, you might choose to discuss it with them to deepen your understanding and generate ideas for critiquing the material. Alternatively, make notes about the main message and methods in the source so you are clear about both the content and the approach.

Here is an illustration of how important it is to understand a source before you paraphrase an extract. The following passage is from an article by Marsh called 'Turnitin.com and the Scriptural Enterprise of Plagiarism Detection' (2004). Marsh points out that plagiarism is often associated with immorality and he critiques this view in his article. Read the extract below and note the features identified by the arrows.

Marsh does not agree with the
view that plagiarised texts are
unhealthy in contrast to healthy
original texts [emphasis added]

Marsh critiques the view that
plagiarism is an abuse

Turnitin.com and the Scriptural Enterprise of Plagiarism Detection

Plagiarized texts, the story usually goes, are inherently diseased, different, immoral, and aberrant within a scriptural economy that favors the healthy, original, creative work.

(Marsh 2004: 436)

Although Marsh disagrees with the view reported here that plagiarised texts are un-wholesome, if this extract were read out of context it could easily be misunderstood and the irony in Marsh's remark might be missed. So, before paraphrasing passages you should aim to ensure the following:

- **Make sure you understand the main argument of the text**
- **Ensure you have chosen to paraphrase a passage for a good reason (rather than quote or summarise it).**

Paraphrased passages should usually be integrated into an essay with a clear introduction to the source and a comment about the value in relation to the argument you are making. See Chapter 9 for tips on synthesising sources into your own argument with an element of critique.

PREPARING TO PARAPHRASE

Once you have checked your understanding of a passage in the wider context of the source, you should prepare to paraphrase by making notes about the author's key points. For example, if you were paraphrasing the above extract from Marsh's article (2004), you might jot down the points as shown in the box below.

Notes on Marsh (2004: 436)

Some scholars argue that plagiarised texts are:

- diseased
- different
- immoral
- aberrant

this can be contrasted with a conception of

- healthy
- original
- creative work.

[Marsh sets up this contrast between bad and good texts.]

List of references entry

Marsh, B. (2004) Turnitin.com and the Scriptural Enterprise of Plagiarism Detection. *Computers and Composition.* **21**: 427–38 (p. 436).

Next, you should try to put the ideas into your own words based on your notes. For instance, you might re-phrase the extract from Marsh's article (2004) in this way:

The meaning of the passage remains as close as possible to Marsh's article but different words have been used

There are many ways of re-phrasing texts and a range of other terms could have been used here

Note that the page number is given because the paraphrase comes from a specific page in the source

> **Paraphrase of Marsh (2004: 436)**
>
> Critics have portrayed plagiarised texts as unhealthy, inappropriate, wrong, and erroneous from a perspective of composition that pro-motes the idea of a wholesome, innovative, new text (Marsh 2004: 436).

Note that the length of this paraphrase is approximately the same as the passage in Marsh's article. You should try to capture the sense of the passage in your source and maintain the length when you paraphrase. If you do not find this easy, remember that the more you practise paraphrasing the better you will become (Neville 2007: 36).

Where does the punctuation go?

Notice that in the example above the full stop comes at the end of the sentence after the in-text citation. You should observe the usual practice in the scholarly sources recommended by your tutors and remember that the appropriate punctuation for paraphrases depends on the context and the specific guidelines in your chosen referencing style. If you use a numerical referencing system, for instance, the full stop goes at the end of the sentence before the superscript number, like this.[1]

SUMMARY

This chapter has given the rationale for paraphrasing and explained how to para-phrase and acknowledge your sources using in-text citations. It has pointed out that you need to understand texts fully before deciding to borrow material, and has stressed that paraphrases must be introduced and integrated into your writ-ing with comment as appropriate.

The main arguments in this chapter:

- Choose passages to paraphrase with care
- Vary paraphrasing with quoting and summarising
- Acknowledge the sources you paraphrase, usually including the page numbers.

[1] This is an example of where to punctuate when using a numerical referencing style.

QUIZ

Read the extract below from Marsh (2004). Which of these examples paraphrase and cite accurately, and which are inaccurate? Can you identify why?

Turnitin.com and the Scriptural Enterprise of Plagiarism Detection

[P]lagiarism detection solutions – which build on the assumption that plagiarism by definition represents a false or mistaken authorship – inherently cast plagiarists as significantly different from other categorically true writers.

(Marsh 2004: 430)

---

1 Is this paraphrase and citation accurate?

Example 1

Software for identifying instances of plagiarism, which operates on the understanding that plagiarism is a kind of crime, represents writers who plagiarise as being unlike honest authors (Marsh 2004: 430).

2 Is this paraphrase and citation accurate?

Example 2

Plagiarism identification tools encourage the belief that plagiarism is a false or mistaken authorship, and they cast plagiarists as significantly different from other categorically genuine writers (p. 430).

3 Is this paraphrase and citation accurate?

Example 3

Software for identifying instances of plagiarism (Marsh), which operates on the understanding that plagiarism is a kind of crime, represents writers who plagiarise as being unlike honest authors.

4 Is this paraphrase and citation accurate?

Example 4

Plagiarism identification tools are problematic for use in higher education.

5 Is this paraphrase and citation accurate?

> ## Example 5
>
> Plagiarism is not necessarily a crime according to Marsh (2004: 430) because sometimes writers copy by accident.

PRACTICE

Here is an example for you to practise paraphrasing. The following passage is from an article by Sorapure *et al.* called 'Web Literacy: Challenges and Opportunities for Research in a New Medium' (1998). Here the authors describe the purpose of academic research:

> ## Web Literacy: Challenges and Opportunities for Research in a New Medium
>
> Research, broadly conceived, involves not only finding relevant information but also assessing its quality and value for a specific project, and then determining how to integrate that information, together with other sources, into one's own writing.
>
> (Sorapure *et al.* 1998: 410)

Try making your own notes about the ideas in this passage; for instance, you might jot down:

> **Scholarly enquiry, in general terms, means:**
> * locating useful sources
> * and
> * evaluating them in relation to a particular task.
>   In addition, it involves:
> * assessing how to synthesise the material alongside other information into a text.

When you have made some notes, write a paraphrase of the extract and cite appropriately. You could ask a friend to read your paraphrase to identify whether it is clear and accurate.

Tips

- If you cannot think of synonyms (other words meaning the same as the terms used by Sorapure et al.), you could try looking up the words in a printed or online thesaurus to find suggestions of alternatives.

- Remember that you should preserve the length and structure of the passage so it means the same, although you have expressed the ideas in your own words. Do not forget that you can summarise sources if you wish to be more concise than paraphrasing will allow, and there are tips on this in the next chapter.

8 INTEGRATING SOURCES BY SUMMARISING

This chapter explains how to summarise and cite sources in your academic writing. It discusses how to introduce and integrate summaries of different types into your writing and how to analyse sources as appropriate.

The chapter covers:

- Summarising sources
- Acknowledging sources
- In-text citations
- Different types of summaries
- Selecting sections to summarise
- When to give page numbers in your in-text citations.

Using this chapter

INTRODUCTION

Having explained how to paraphrase in the previous chapter, Chapter 8 shows how you can integrate sources into your own writing by summarising. It discusses different type of summaries and explains when you need to give page numbers in your in-text citations.

SUMMARISING

To summarise a source means to give a brief account of the points that are relevant for your own writing. Summaries are usually much shorter than the original text, so summarising material is an efficient way to demonstrate your knowledge and understanding of a wide range of sources (Lunsford 2008: 265).

When you are writing for assessment, try to balance your use of quoting and paraphrasing with summarising in order to create variety in your use of sources. In many instances, summarising is **more** appropriate than either quoting or paraphrasing because it enables you to capture relevant points from whole texts or large sections of the sources you read.

Acknowledging your sources

When you summarise sources you must give an in-text citation stating the author's surname and the date of the source. You only need to give the page number if you summarise an extract from a particular page, or if you think readers may want to locate the exact passage. In addition to this in-text citation you must give the full publication details in your list of references in accordance with your chosen referencing style. Below is an example of a summary with an in-text citation in the Harvard style. This is a summary of an article by Gornall called 'Whistleblowing: The Price of Silence' (2009).

Summary with in-text citation in the Harvard style

Gornall's article 'Whistleblowing: The Price of Silence' (2009) discusses the pressures on health workers not to speak out about poor standards of care. He provides a range of examples of professionals at hospitals across Britain who were silenced when they raised causes for concern. Gornall contrasts this reality with the rhetoric from politicians and hospital managers and discusses the pros and cons of 'gagging clauses' which can be used to cover up mistakes or protect employees from the consequences of errors. Gornall identifies the obligation of health professionals to raise awareness about failures, but he points out that it is not always possible to change systems from within. His concluding reminder is that healthcare professionals are expected to put patients first and he implies that doctors should monitor policies to achieve this aim.

Here is an example of the accompanying entry in the list of references at the end of the writing:

Gornall, J. (2009) Whistleblowing: The Price of Silence. *British Medical Journal* **339**: 1000–4.

Why summarise sources?

Summarising is a valuable means of demonstrating your ability to read critically and select the points in a source which are most pertinent for your own writing. It is not easy to identify which ideas are the most relevant for your purpose, so the ability to summarise is highly valued within academia. In choosing an aspect of a source to summarise you not only demonstrate insight into that text but also show that you are in control of your own writing by judging the best evidence to use.

HOW TO SUMMARISE SOURCES

Before attempting to write a summary you should make sure the text is appropriate for your piece of writing. Read your source carefully and check you fully understand the argument that is being made. The next task is to choose how much text you want to capture. Depending on the extent of the material that is relevant for you there are two main types of summary:

1 A summary of an *entire* source such as a journal article, chapter, or book
2 A summary of a *single* point, passage, or section within a source such as a paragraph or a page.

SUMMARISING AN ENTIRE SOURCE

Summarising an entire source is quite demanding, but remember that you can take a particular angle on the material and your summary should be much shorter than the source (Lunsford 2008: 266). When you summarise an entire source you should not give the page numbers in your in-text citations because you are referring to the whole text.

You cannot summarise until you have read and understood the text in full, so leave yourself time to do this properly. The best way to improve at writing summaries is to practise and you can pick up tips from seeing how academics summarise scholarly journal articles. Scholarly journal articles are prefaced by a short synopsis of the argument called the 'abstract', which is an example of a summary of an entire source.

Below is the abstract for an article by Howard called 'Understanding "Internet Plagiarism"' (2007). Read Howard's abstract and note the features identified by the arrows.

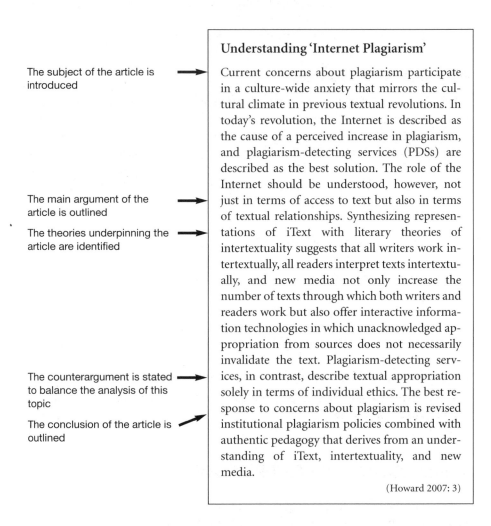

The subject of the article is introduced ➡

The main argument of the article is outlined ➡

The theories underpinning the article are identified ➡

The counterargument is stated to balance the analysis of this topic ➡

The conclusion of the article is outlined ➡

Understanding 'Internet Plagiarism'

Current concerns about plagiarism participate in a culture-wide anxiety that mirrors the cultural climate in previous textual revolutions. In today's revolution, the Internet is described as the cause of a perceived increase in plagiarism, and plagiarism-detecting services (PDSs) are described as the best solution. The role of the Internet should be understood, however, not just in terms of access to text but also in terms of textual relationships. Synthesizing representations of iText with literary theories of intertextuality suggests that all writers work intertextually, all readers interpret texts intertextually, and new media not only increase the number of texts through which both writers and readers work but also offer interactive information technologies in which unacknowledged appropriation from sources does not necessarily invalidate the text. Plagiarism-detecting services, in contrast, describe textual appropriation solely in terms of individual ethics. The best response to concerns about plagiarism is revised institutional plagiarism policies combined with authentic pedagogy that derives from an understanding of iText, intertextuality, and new media.

(Howard 2007: 3)

Howard's abstract summarises a 17-page article, but you could write an even more concise synopsis of this source by considering the same five features highlighted here. See the summary below for an example of a more concise synopsis.

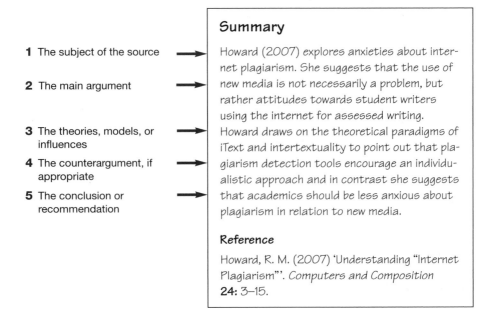

Summary

Howard (2007) explores anxieties about internet plagiarism. She suggests that the use of new media is not necessarily a problem, but rather attitudes towards student writers using the internet for assessed writing. Howard draws on the theoretical paradigms of iText and intertextuality to point out that plagiarism detection tools encourage an individualistic approach and in contrast she suggests that academics should be less anxious about plagiarism in relation to new media.

1 The subject of the source

2 The main argument

3 The theories, models, or influences

4 The counterargument, if appropriate

5 The conclusion or recommendation

Reference

Howard, R. M. (2007) 'Understanding "Internet Plagiarism"'. *Computers and Composition* **24**: 3–15.

The key when summarising an entire source is to consider carefully which aspects are most relevant for your own writing. You do not have to mention every point made by an author so you may choose to focus on the theoretical framework, for instance. You might summarise this theory and apply it in a different context for your own work. Alternatively, you may be interested in the conclusions drawn in a source, which you could discuss and build upon for your own purpose. Here is an alternative, shorter summary of Howard's article:

Howard (2007) identifies theories that illuminate the issue of internet plagiarism, namely iText and intertextuality.

SUMMARISING A SECTION WITHIN A SOURCE

You can choose part of a source to summarise depending on your interests and the task you are working on. When you summarise material from a specific page you should usually include the *page number* in your in-text citation; check this with your tutor if you are unsure.

Selecting points that are appropriate for your own writing may mean ignoring the majority of a text, and this requires careful critical reading to identify the most relevant material. The extract below is taken from Howard's article 'Understanding

"Internet Plagiarism"' (2007). Look at this extract and the summary of this section of the article below:

Understanding 'Internet Plagiarism'

Although the word *plagiarism* dates back to the Rome of the poet Martial, the idea of plagiarism and its opposite, originality, as significant textual principles date from the eighteenth century and specifically from the monetary opportunities provided by the printing press. It was London booksellers who agitated for copyright, and it was their supporters who justified it on the basis of a contrast between plagiarism and originality.

(Howard 2007: 7)

From the extract above you might be interested in Howard's discussion of historical influences on contemporary conceptions of plagiarism. From this angle your summary of this section of the article might be:

Howard points out the ancient roots of the word plagiarism, but she also highlights the development of originality as a concept in the eighteenth century (2007: 7).

SUMMARY

This chapter has provided the rationale for summarising and explained how to summarise whole texts as well as sections of texts. It has emphasised that summaries of whole texts do not require page numbers for the in-text citations, whereas summaries of short sections of text usually require page numbers for the in-text citations. Always check your recommended referencing style and ask your tutor if you are unsure about this.

The main arguments in this chapter:

- Choose passages to summarise with care
- Decide whether to summarise the whole text or a short section
- Vary summarising with quoting and paraphrasing
- Acknowledge the sources you summarise, usually including the page numbers for short sections.

QUIZ

Read the extract below from Howard (2007). Which of these examples summarise and cite accurately, and which are inaccurate? Can you identify why?

Understanding 'Internet Plagiarism'

Although today mass literacy is widely regarded as a universal social good, in the nineteenth century it was greeted with wide skepticism. John Trimbur (2000) noted that many members of the upper class regarded popular literacy with suspicion; it had the potential to fuel discontent and even revolution (p. 287).

(Howard 2007: 6)

---

1 Is this summary and citation accurate?

Example 1

In contemporary society literacy for the masses is recognised as desirable but this was not the case in the nineteenth century (Howard 2007: 6). This point was made in 2000 by Trimbur (cited in Howard 2007: 6) who pointed out that during that period the upper classes were not in favour of mass education owing to fears of insurrection.

---

2 Is this summary and citation accurate?

Example 2

Howard argues that there is a difference between attitudes towards literacy today and several hundred years ago (6).

---

3 Is this summary and citation accurate?

Example 3

The ability to read and write is acknowledged as an advantage today but in the nineteenth century not everyone agreed (Howard 2007: 6).

4 Is this summary and citation accurate?

Example 4

According to Trimbur the upper classes were suspicious of literacy in the nineteenth century.

---

5 Is this summary and citation accurate?

Example 5

The ability to read and write has not always been appreciated by society (2007).

---

9 ▶ CRITIQUING SOURCES

This chapter explains how to critique and cite sources in your academic writing. It stresses the importance of critical thinking and demonstrates how to build upon existing research to make original points in your writing.

The chapter covers:

- Critiquing sources
- Acknowledging sources
- In-text citations
- Questions for critiquing sources
- Drawing on research to make your own points
- Examples of critiques.

Using this chapter

INTRODUCTION

Having explained how to quote, paraphrase, and summarise in the previous chapters, Chapter 9 shows how you can build upon these techniques to critique sources as you integrate them into your own writing.

CRITIQUING

To critique a source means to point out the strengths and weaknesses in relation to the topic you are writing about. The advantage of critiquing the sources you integrate into your own work is that it allows you to put your own stamp on material and build upon other people's ideas to generate fresh perspectives and analyses (Sopure *et al*. 1998: 40). Sometimes writers critique existing research to identify gaps and put forward their own argument to fill these gaps. As you approach any text, ask yourself the following four questions to develop your critical thinking:

1 *Who* wrote this source and on what authority?
2 *Why* has this source been written?
3 *When* was this source written?
4 *What* does this source reveal that is useful to me? (Can I identify any limitations and put forward points of my own?)

These four questions, beginning *who*, *why*, *when*, and *what*, will become increasingly easy to answer as you practise critiquing sources. If you keep them in mind when you are reading and respond as appropriate within your writing you will boost the level of analysis within your work.

Acknowledging your sources

When you critique sources you must give an in-text citation stating the author's surname and the date of the source. You only need to give the page number if you critique an extract from a particular page or you think readers may want to locate the exact passage. In addition to this in-text citation you must give the full publication details in your list of references in accordance with your chosen referencing style. Below is an example of a critique with an in-text citation in the Harvard style. This passage critiques an article by Gornall called 'Whistleblowing: The Price of Silence' (2009).

> Gornall's article 'Whistleblowing: The Price of Silence' (2009) is effective in identifying the consequences when health professionals raise the alarm about problematic structures, systems, and policies within the National Health Service. His survey of recent incidents sheds light on the complexities of this topic and his coverage of legal issues is informative. However, a comparative analysis with contexts beyond the UK would have enhanced the discussion.

Here is an example of the accompanying entry in the list of references at the end of the writing:

Gornall, J. (2009) Whistleblowing: The Price of Silence. *British Medical Journal* **339:** 1000–4.

WHY CRITIQUE SOURCES?

The main reason for critiquing sources is to build upon existing research to generate ideas of your own (Barnet and Bedau 2008: 116). In fact it can be difficult to come up with fresh thoughts about a subject without engaging with what scholars have already argued, so you should use the literature in your field to help spark innovative approaches and interpretations.

Validate your writing

Critiquing sources demonstrates that you know what scholars have argued about your topic and that you can engage critically with their ideas. Pointing out the applications, implications, or limitations of your sources demands extra effort, but this is well worth the trouble because analysis raises the quality of your work.

Enhance your written style

Another benefit of critiquing sources is that this can inform your own use of language. If you are attentive to the structure of texts and scholars' use of language, you can identify how experts discuss ideas to become more adept at producing the conventions associated with your discipline. As you read scholarly sources, try to keep a note of the qualities you appreciate so you can try these out in your own writing. Be careful not to copy ideas or words without acknowledging the source by giving an in-text citation and making an entry in your list of references in accordance with your chosen referencing style.

HOW TO CRITIQUE SOURCES

You usually need to quote, paraphrase, or summarise a source before you can critique it to give readers enough information to make sense of your critique. Before critiquing a source or a short extract, check that you fully understand the purpose of the whole text. Although effective analysis can enhance your authority as a writer, if you misinterpret information you can undermine your credibility.

Drawing on a variety of sources to develop your own ideas

As you critique sources do not forget the aim of your own writing and make your comments relevant to this. Usually you will want to use existing literature as a springboard to move from what others have argued to develop your own points and perspectives. Below are some examples of how to build upon sources to develop your own ideas.

Critiquing example A

This example is taken from an article by Howard called 'Understanding "Internet Plagiarism"' (2007). Howard surveys the literature on the history of printing and the introduction of widespread education in Britain. Read the extract below and note the features identified by the arrows.

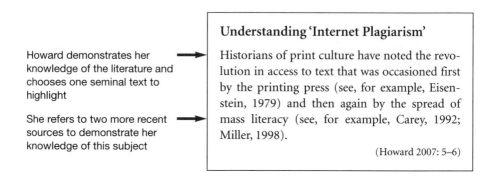

Howard demonstrates her knowledge of the literature and chooses one seminal text to highlight

She refers to two more recent sources to demonstrate her knowledge of this subject

Understanding 'Internet Plagiarism'

Historians of print culture have noted the revolution in access to text that was occasioned first by the printing press (see, for example, Eisenstein, 1979) and then again by the spread of mass literacy (see, for example, Carey, 1992; Miller, 1998).

(Howard 2007: 5–6)

In critiquing example A Howard does not critique these sources or build upon them to make her own points, but she does this effectively in example B.

Critiquing example B

The second example is also taken from Howard's article (2007). Here she discusses influential theories about writing and the meaning of plagiarism. Read this extract and note the features identified by the arrows.

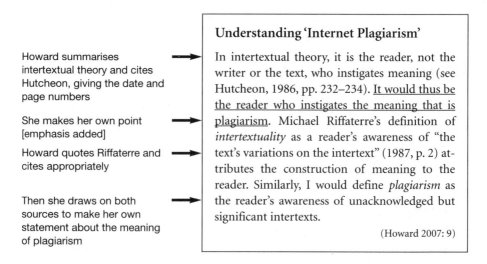

Howard summarises intertextual theory and cites Hutcheon, giving the date and page numbers

She makes her own point [emphasis added]

Howard quotes Riffaterre and cites appropriately

Then she draws on both sources to make her own statement about the meaning of plagiarism

Understanding 'Internet Plagiarism'

In intertextual theory, it is the reader, not the writer or the text, who instigates meaning (see Hutcheon, 1986, pp. 232–234). It would thus be the reader who instigates the meaning that is plagiarism. Michael Riffaterre's definition of intertextuality as a reader's awareness of "the text's variations on the intertext" (1987, p. 2) attributes the construction of meaning to the reader. Similarly, I would define plagiarism as the reader's awareness of unacknowledged but significant intertexts.

(Howard 2007: 9)

In your own writing, try to emulate this technique of commenting upon existing literature to develop your own points. Notice that citing these scholars appropriately gives Howard authority when she advances her own argument.

Critiquing example C

The third example is taken from an article by DeVoss and Rosati called '"It Wasn't Me, Was It?" Plagiarism and the Web' (2002). In this extract the authors not only integrate sources into their argument, but also comment on the value of these texts in relation to their discussion of internet plagiarism. Read this extract and note the features identified by the arrows.

DeVoss and Rosati critique a source by Burton and Chadwick (they have already cited this source)

They identify a limitation with the source

DeVoss and Rosati use this gap in the literature to introduce their own original ideas

'It Wasn't Me, Was It?' Plagiarism and the Web

Burton and Chadwick provide an excellent analysis of Internet research, but, like many other authors addressing issues of Internet research, do not discuss issues of plagiarism. Here we offer two approaches that apply to both offline and online research and writing – supplements crucial to our first-year composition classes if we are to successfully integrate web work into our curricula, a choice not up to us to make as more and more students rely on the Web as a research space and as more and more institutions adopt web-based teaching interfaces (like WebCT, Blackboard, and Daedalus Online).

(DeVoss et al. 2002: 198)

In your own writing, where it is appropriate, try to emulate this technique of identifying gaps in existing research and propose ways to fill the gaps.

Critiquing example D

The fourth example is taken from the same article by DeVoss and Rosati (2002). Here they make a point about helping student writers to avoid plagiarism and support the point by citing a number of sources. Read this extract and note the features identified by the arrows.

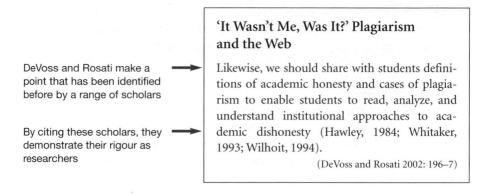

DeVoss and Rosati make a point that has been identified before by a range of scholars

> **'It Wasn't Me, Was It?' Plagiarism and the Web**
>
> Likewise, we should share with students definitions of academic honesty and cases of plagiarism to enable students to read, analyze, and understand institutional approaches to academic dishonesty (Hawley, 1984; Whitaker, 1993; Wilhoit, 1994).
>
> (DeVoss and Rosati 2002: 196–7)

By citing these scholars, they demonstrate their rigour as researchers

In your own writing, try to demonstrate your knowledge of the literature and cite appropriately following your chosen referencing style.

Critiquing example E

The fifth example is also taken from the article by DeVoss and Rosati (2002). Here they make the related point that breaking down assessment tasks for student writers can help to reduce plagiarism. They support this by citing a number of sources. Read this extract and note the features identified by the arrows.

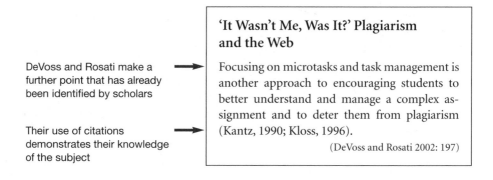

DeVoss and Rosati make a further point that has already been identified by scholars

> **'It Wasn't Me, Was It?' Plagiarism and the Web**
>
> Focusing on microtasks and task management is another approach to encouraging students to better understand and manage a complex assignment and to deter them from plagiarism (Kantz, 1990; Kloss, 1996).
>
> (DeVoss and Rosati 2002: 197)

Their use of citations demonstrates their knowledge of the subject

In your own writing, where it is appropriate, try to back up points with citations in a similar way to establish your authority on a topic.

Critiquing example F

This final example is taken from the same article and it shows that, having established credibility by citing relevant literature, DeVoss and Rosati successfully advance their own argument. Read this extract and note the features identified by the arrows.

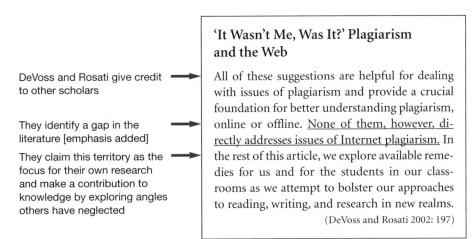

DeVoss and Rosati give credit to other scholars →

They identify a gap in the literature [emphasis added] →

They claim this territory as the focus for their own research and make a contribution to knowledge by exploring angles others have neglected →

'It Wasn't Me, Was It?' Plagiarism and the Web

All of these suggestions are helpful for dealing with issues of plagiarism and provide a crucial foundation for better understanding plagiarism, online or offline. <u>None of them, however, directly addresses issues of Internet plagiarism.</u> In the rest of this article, we explore available remedies for us and for the students in our classrooms as we attempt to bolster our approaches to reading, writing, and research in new realms.

(DeVoss and Rosati 2002: 197)

SUMMARY

This chapter has provided the rationale for critiquing and explained how to critique sources as you integrate them into your own writing. It has demonstrated how to build upon existing research to make your own points and stressed the need to cite and reference using your chosen referencing style.

The main arguments in this chapter:

- Identify limitations in your sources, if appropriate
- Build upon existing literature to advance your own ideas, if appropriate
- Acknowledge the sources you critique, including the page numbers for short sections.

PART 4

REFERENCING

INTRODUCTION TO PART 4

Part 4 demonstrates how to cite and reference in the Harvard style, which is a popular and simple system used in many disciplines to document sources (Neville 2007: 49). Before adopting this style, you must **check that it is the recommended referencing system** for your subject by asking your tutors or consulting the handbooks and guidance you have been given.

There are lots of slightly different variations of the Harvard style because, unlike other referencing systems, there is no official publication on this style. Instead, a variety of websites and handbooks offer slightly differing advice, which can be very confusing. So, in Part 4 emphasis is placed on *why* sources are cited and referenced to help you understand the rationale for acknowledging sources with care. Advice is also provided on ways of remembering how to cite and reference different types of sources. This will help you develop a clear and consistent approach to acknowledging your sources, but you should also consult your tutors for advice.

Chapter 10 explains how to cite materials in the Harvard style and suggests ways of remembering how to format different types of sources in the list of references. Chapter 11 introduces other referencing systems and the disciplines in which they are often adopted.

Part 4 is designed to help you gain confidence so you can acknowledge sources with consistency and clarity, whichever referencing system or version of the Harvard style you adopt. The main message of the following two chapters is that you need to learn the conventions for citing and referencing in your subject area, and **practise** until these become automatic. Remember:

1 Referencing conventions are distinctive in each subject area

2 Every scholar must learn how to cite and reference in the appropriate style

3 Most scholars learn to use multiple referencing styles.

This chapter demonstrates how to use the Harvard style and provides a wide range of examples. The chapter stresses the importance of clear and consistent acknowledgement of sources, and points out that you need to use your own judgement when you are acknowledging unusual sources.

The chapter covers:

- Variations of the Harvard style
- In-text citations
- The list of references
- Written sources
- Secondary sources
- Numerical sources
- Audiovisual sources
- Digital formats.

Using this chapter

INTRODUCTION

This chapter explains how to cite and reference using the Harvard style. However, before adopting any referencing system you must consult the guidance given to you by your tutors and follow their advice. Course handbooks and assignment briefs usually specify which style you should use, and if in doubt you should ask your tutors or seek advice at your university library.

VARIATIONS OF THE HARVARD STYLE

There is no single version of the Harvard style because there is no official publication providing instructions on how to use this referencing system. Instead, you will find many different websites and manuals which all give slightly different advice. The existence of different versions of the Harvard style can create confusion because each version recommends slightly different use of punctuation, and sometimes different ways of formatting the pieces of information required for list of reference entries. For example, you may be advised to insert a comma after the author's surname, or write 'p.' instead of a colon before giving page numbers.

Do not let the existence of different variations of the Harvard style confuse you, but choose a version in consultation with your tutors and stick with it. The main aim of referencing is to show readers **where you have borrowed material from sources**, and, as long as this information is *clear and consistently formatted* you will be successful as a scholar and researcher.

TWO ELEMENTS

Whichever version of the Harvard style you use, there are two elements you need to master (Williams and Carron 2009: 7). The two elements are:

1 *In-text citations* every time you borrow material from a source
2 A *list of references* at the end of your work.

Your academic writing must contain both in-text citations and a list of references. In-text citations are acknowledgements of the author, date, and when appropriate the page number each time you borrow from a source. You should place in-text citations within brackets and insert a colon before the page number like this:

> Academic writing involves 'careful citation and critical thinking' (McArthur 2010: 5).

It is a serious omission not to cite the sources you refer to in your writing, and this omission constitutes *plagiarism* because it is a failure to acknowledge authors' intellectual property.

There are various ways of integrating sources into your own writing. When you borrow numerical data or images you should introduce these clearly, and if appropriate label them as figures or tables. When borrowing words and ideas, you can quote, paraphrase, summarise, and critique sources (Neville 2007: 36). Whichever method you choose to integrate sources into your own writing, you must give *an in-text citation* to acknowledge the material you borrow.

As mentioned above, in addition to your in-text citations you must make a list recording more information for each source you have cited. The most challenging aspect of referencing is to **learn the formula** for formatting different types of sources such as books, journal articles, and websites, but with practice this becomes increasingly easy.

IN-TEXT CITATIONS

As previously mentioned, the term 'in-text citation' means an acknowledgement of your sources each time you borrow material for your writing. The Harvard style is easy to use because you simply cite the author's surname, the date, and when appropriate the page numbers in brackets. When you borrow images or statistics, and when you quote, paraphrase, or summarise a short passage, you should usually give the page number. Here is an example:

Give the author's surname and the date, then insert a colon and give the page number enclosed within brackets ➝ (Jones 2010: 34)

Here is another example:

The role of academic writing in assessment at university

Accuracy and agility as a writer are essential to obtain good grades at university (Smith 2010: 4). According to Shah (2009: 7) strong written communication is one of the determining factors in success at this advanced level.

This example shows that each time you borrow from a source you should give the author's surname and date, plus the **page number if you refer to a specific page**. You can either name the authors in your own sentence, or give their surnames within your in-text citations, and you can vary this depending on the emphasis you want to give.

How to cite

You need to gather three pieces of information when you are making notes to produce accurate in-text citations. Ask yourself:

1 Who is the *author*?

If there are multiple authors, write them all down in your notes. If the author is an organisation or group of people this is known as the **corporate author**.

2 In which *year* was the source published?

If the source is digital, when was it last updated?

3 Do you need to give *page numbers*?

You usually do if you quote, paraphrase, summarise an extract from a specific page, borrow data, or use images from printed sources. Ask your tutor if you are unsure.

CITING WRITTEN SOURCES

You should also take note of the ways authors cite material in journal articles because these often provide models for academic writing in your own discipline. In particular, notice how authors integrate quotes, paraphrases, summaries, and critiques of sources as they develop their own ideas.

Multiple authors

It can be disruptive for readers if you cite a source with many authors because this interrupts the flow of your own writing. To avoid this, the convention when one source has many authors is to give the first author's surname, then use the Latin term 'et al.' which is an abbreviation of et alii meaning 'and others'. Note that you must insert a full stop after 'et al.' because it is an abbreviated term. Here is an example:

> Gillett et al. argue that writing is a core capability at university (2009: 54).

Remember that although you are writing one author's surname you are actually referring to multiple authors, so your own sentence must agree grammatically. It is inaccurate to write 'Gillett et al. argue<u>s</u>' because you are referring to authors in the plural, so your own verb must agree.

Variations of the Harvard style give different recommendations about when to use 'et al.' and how to format this term. A common approach is to use et al. when there are more than *two* authors. However, some variations of the Harvard style recommend using et al. when there are more than three authors. Similarly, some variations of the Harvard style require you to italicise *et al.* thus because it is a Latin term and foreign phrases are often italicised in academic writing.

The examples below offer further advice on using in-text citations in the Harvard style.

Mentioning authors at the start of sentences

You can refer to an author directly and cite the source near the start of your sentence like this:

McCutcheon (2010: 43) argues that academic writing cannot be taught generically, but must be explored as an 'integral part' of disciplinary studies.

Mentioning authors at the end of sentences

Alternatively, you can refer to an author directly and cite the source near the end of your sentence so it does not disrupt the flow of your argument, like this:

McCutcheon argues that academic writing cannot be taught generically, but must be explored as an 'integral part' of disciplinary studies (2010: 43).

Giving authors within in-text citations

You can give the author's name in your in-text citation rather than in your own sentence like this:

Academic writing cannot be taught generically, but must be explored as an 'integral part' of disciplinary studies (McCutcheon 2010: 43).

As you will see when you read scholarly journal articles, authors tend to use all three approaches in their writing. Notice the most common way of citing in your subject area and adopt this, but also feel free to vary these three techniques to suit your own written style.

Citing more than one source

Be careful if you refer to more than one source in a single sentence because you must ensure that your readers can identify which author has made which point. Look at the two examples of citing below. Which is clearer?

Example 1: many citations in a list

> Recent research into road safety recommends a revised approach to teaching children how to cross roads through national education programmes and local initiatives (Anderson 2000: 3, Potter 2001: 54, Scott 2003: 6, Jones and Sharma 2009: 87).

In the example above, the writer has cited four sources in one sentence so the reader is unclear what each source is about.

Example 2: many citations clearly distinguished

> Recent research into road safety recommends a revised approach to teaching children how to cross roads through national education programmes (Potter 2001: 54, Scott 2003: 6) and local initiatives (Anderson 2000: 3, Jones and Sharma 2009: 87).

In the second example the writer has listed only two sources in each in-text citation so that readers are much clearer which authors made which points. When you are citing sources try to make it clear who made which point and avoid listing many texts at once because this can confuse readers. If your in-text citations are precise they are more helpful for readers who are interested in your topic.

The order for listing citations

When you list a number of citations in one sentence you should think about the order. Check the guidelines in your chosen referencing style and be consistent. Notice that in the example above, the citations are given in chronological order with the oldest first. Some referencing styles recommend listing the most recent source first, so check with your tutor if you are unsure.

Page numbers and in-text citations

Every time you quote, paraphrase, or summarise a short section you should usually give the page number, unless you are using a digital source that does not contain page numbers.

The same applies when you borrow *images* or *numerical data*. Basically, whenever you borrow from a particular page your readers may need to know the page number to locate that page for themselves. However, check with your tutor as practice can vary in different disciplines.

There are three main reasons for giving page numbers. First, it demonstrates your professionalism and conveys your ability to make notes in a scholarly way. Secondly, it helps readers track down the passages, images, and data you have borrowed and consult this information themselves. Thirdly, examiners may want to check you have understood a source, and they will not be impressed if you do not leave a clear account of exactly where in your source you have referenced. In general, omitting page numbers gives an impression of laziness, so avoid this by jotting down the page numbers when you are making notes, and include them in your in-text citations whenever you quote, paraphrase or refer to a specific page.

Why give page numbers?

1 To show professionalism
2 To help readers track down the passages, images, and data you have borrowed
3 To meet marking criteria and show examiners you can cite in a scholarly fashion.

Page numbers and paraphrasing

Most versions of the Harvard style advise you to give page numbers when you paraphrase a passage from a source. This is because, although when you paraphrase you put an author's ideas into your own words, borrowing material in this way is not very different from quoting.

Page numbers and summarising

There are two different ways of summarising material; one of which is to summarise the whole source, and the other is to summarise a short section of a source. If you summarise an entire book or journal article you do not need to provide the page numbers in your in-text citations. However, if you summarise a specific passage you should give the page number in case readers wish to locate the passage. You will need to use your judgement when deciding whether or not to give page numbers, but it is better to give pages unnecessarily than to omit them when they are required. In particular, some examiners may penalise writers who quote without giving the page numbers.

CITING SECONDARY SOURCES

Secondary sources are sources cited in the texts you read. They are 'secondary' because you have not seen them yourself. If you can locate the original sources and cite them as usual this demonstrates your research skills. As secondary sources are sometimes reported inaccurately, locating them for yourself helps you avoid bringing errors into your work.

However, if you are unable to locate the original source, you must make it clear to readers that you are citing a source you have not seen. To cite a secondary source, give the author of the secondary source and the date, then write 'cited in' and give the author, date and page number of the source you have read. Here is an example of citing a secondary source:

> Academic writing demands time, planning, and commitment (Adams 2007 cited in Downs 2010: 34).

CITING NUMERICAL SOURCES

Give an in-text citation acknowledging the author or statistician each time you borrow statistics, graphs or other numerical data from sources. Follow the same basic practice for citing numerical data as you would for citing written sources. You will often have to make a judgement about who to cite as the author, and this will depend on the purpose of your writing. Here is an example of citing statistics:

> A recent survey indicates that 24% of pet owners rescued their animals from homes or charities (Pets Research 2010: 32).

When you borrow numerical data from a specific page in a printed source you should give the *page number* so readers can locate the same place in the source with ease.

Depending on the nature of your writing, it may be useful to put numerical data into a table. This is particularly appropriate if you are writing a substantial piece of work such as a report, dissertation or thesis. If you do this you should give the figure a title and produce a contents page for your document, including a list of figures. Remember to discuss the significance of the data (see Figure 10.1).

CITING AUDIOVISUAL SOURCES

Just as you integrate written sources into your writing using different techniques such as quoting, paraphrasing, summarising, and critiquing, you should also integrate audiovisual sources into your writing in a scholarly fashion. Figure 10.1 shows how to cite numerical data.

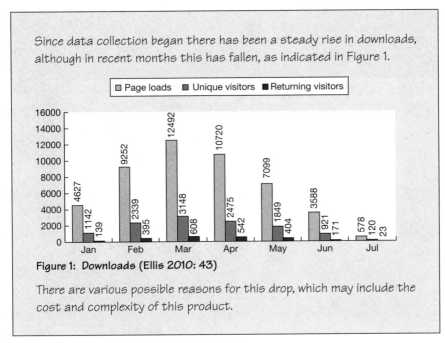

Since data collection began there has been a steady rise in downloads, although in recent months this has fallen, as indicated in Figure 1.

Figure 1: Downloads (Ellis 2010: 43)

There are various possible reasons for this drop, which may include the cost and complexity of this product.

Figure 10.1 Numerical data

Always assess the value of sources before borrowing from them for your work and be clear about the purpose they serve. Remember to give the page number when you borrow data and images from printed sources.

Introduce each audiovisual source as you introduce it into your writing and comment on it as appropriate. If you are writing a substantial document such as a report, dissertation, or thesis you should label the images as figures and include a list of figures in your list of contents. Figure 10.2 shows how to cite visual sources.

Citing films, videos, and DVDs (not downloaded)

For this type of source you need to decide who to cite as the author, and most commonly it is appropriate to cite the director or producer. Here is an example of citing a DVD:

In *Cold Mountain*, Kidman brings the American Civil War to life (Minghella 2004).

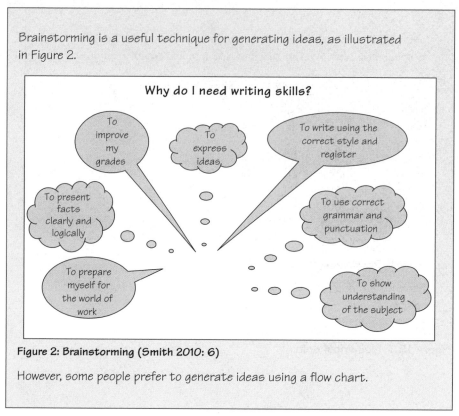

Figure 10.2 **Visual sources**

CITING DIGITAL FORMATS

Many different types of sources are available digitally, so the best way to support you in documenting your digital sources is to provide some general guidelines for you to adopt as appropriate for your different writing projects.

Quality control and online sources

Websites can be very useful as leads for future research; for example, the website Wikipedia is not subject to scholarly review so anyone could make an inaccurate contribution and it would be unfortunate to repeat errors in your own work. On the other hand, the references supplied within Wikipedia articles are potentially valuable if you follow them up and assess their value for your own use.

It is vital to analyse the quality of online sources before you draw on material for your academic writing (Hacker 2006: 31). Some online sources are unreliable or inaccurate and therefore inappropriate for use in academic writing. Be aware, for instance, that translations may not be accurate. The danger of citing unreliable sources is that this can undermine the quality of your own work, so before using online sources, consider whether it is worth consulting more scholarly sources instead.

Corporate authors

If a source is not written by people, but instead is produced by an organisation or professional body, this is known as a 'corporate author'. When citing from sources created by an organisation you should cite the corporate author.

It is not always easy to identify the author of a website, but as long as you give the same details in your in-text citations as in your list of references your readers will be able to locate the source for themselves. This is because your list of references entry will contain the full website address (URL) (see Figure 10.3).

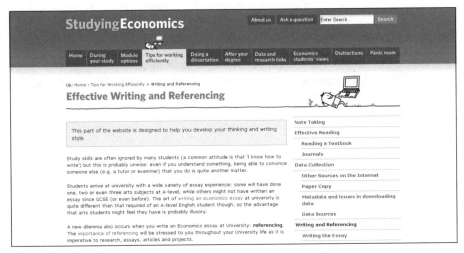

Figure 10.3 Corporate authors

To locate the author of online sources, check the bottom of a webpage to see if there is an acknowledgement or any copyright information. In Figure 10.3, although it is not visible, on this website it says at the bottom of the page:

© The Economics Network of the Higher Education Academy, University of Bristol.

Supported by the Royal Economic Society.

The corporate author here is the Economics Network because the copyright symbol © signals that the intellectual property rights belong to this group. To cite this corporate author you would write:

(Economics Network 2009)

Notice that you do *not* give the website address (URL) within in-text citations because it would disrupt the flow of your own writing. Instead the website address is recorded in your list of references.

Dates and online sources

It is often difficult to find a date within online sources. Check the information at the bottom of the webpage if you cannot see the date at first, and you might find the date when the site was last updated, which you can use for your in-text citations. If no date is given, you can either estimate and give the year you are viewing if recently updated, or write 'n.d.', meaning 'no date', like this:

> (Economics Network n.d.)

Page numbers and online sources

Online sources do not have page numbers, so it is usual practice to omit page numbers for in-text citations of online sources. This is acceptable because readers who wish to locate these sources can use the website address (URL) given in your list of references.

Downloads

Digital media are often available as podcasts and in other formats which allow you to listen to programmes again. To acknowledge these sources when you borrow material for your own writing, you should cite the author and date in brackets. You are the best person to decide which author to cite as you acknowledge your sources, and as long as you link the in-text citations to entries in your list of references your readers will be able to locate the sources for themselves. Below are some examples.

Citing the speaker as author

You can refer directly to the speaker as the author like this:

> As part of the BBC programme *In our time with Melvyn Bragg*, John Haldane discussed the life of St Thomas Aquinas (2009).

Citing the organisation as corporate author

Or, you can refer to the corporate author like this:

> As part of the programme *In our time with Melvyn Bragg*, John Haldane discussed the life of St Thomas Aquinas (BBC Radio 4 2009).

Citing personal communications

To cite a personal communication, quote, paraphrase, or summarise and give the author's surname and the date. Either mention the author in your own writing or in your in-text citation. Here is an example in which the author is mentioned directly:

> In a personal communication Professor Saunders explained his theory in depth (2009).

Citing blogs

To cite a blog, quote, paraphrase, or summarise and give the author's surname and the date. Either mention the author directly, or in your in-text citation. Here is an example in which the author is mentioned in the in-text citation:

> 'This week something great happened: two of my former students connected with me' (Dwyer 2009).

Citing online discussion fora and mailing lists

To cite an online discussion list or listserv, quote, paraphrase, or summarise and give the author's surname and the date. Here is an example in which the author is mentioned in the in-text citation:

> 'Interrogating our approach is essential' (Harris 2009).

Decisions about citing

This section of Chapter 10 has explained how to cite using the Harvard style. It has covered the main points you need to know and recommended that you seek advice from your tutors when you are unsure about any aspect of citing and referencing. It has stressed that there are times when you have to make **decisions** about how to cite sources in your writing. Base these decisions on the following three rules:

1 Be *clear* about where in your writing you have borrowed from sources

2 Be *consistent* as you make choices about which information to cite as the author and date

3 Be *comprehensive* in giving the author, date, and page numbers (when appropriate).

THE LIST OF REFERENCES

A list of references is a full record of all the sources you have cited in your writing. The purpose of this list is to provide all the details readers require to locate your sources for themselves. The example below demonstrates how to produce a list of references.

List of References

Abrahams, B. (2010) *Academic Writing in the United Kingdom*. London: Routledge

Carr, S. (2009) *Writing for success: Assessment in higher education*. Maidstone: HarperCollins

Potter, H. (2005) *An Introduction to Human Anatomy* . 4th edn. London: Adam Arnold available from <http://anatomy/introduction/human/htm> [27th March 2006]

There is a specific format for referencing each different type of source. For printed sources you should record the publication details, and for online sources you should provide the website address and the date you accessed the data.

THE LINK BETWEEN IN-TEXT CITATIONS AND THE LIST OF REFERENCES

As previously mentioned, every source that is given in your in-text citations must be fully recorded in your list of references.

The most efficient way to ensure that all the sources you cite are recorded in your list of references is to compile both elements as you are drafting your work. You should work hard to develop a method that works for you. Many scholars find reference management systems such as EndNote and RefWorks effective for this task (Neville 2007: 23, Williams and Carroll 2009: 78). Ask about these tools at your university library because they can save you lots of time.

How to construct a list of references

The list of references goes at the end of your document and the sources are listed in alphabetical order according to the authors. You should not subdivide this list into types of sources, but you do need to learn how to format the entries for different types of sources. The three main types of source you need to learn about are:

- Books
- Journal articles
- Websites.

Once you have mastered how to reference these three types of sources you will have enough knowledge to reference other source types because they are mostly variations of these three formats.

Use your judgement

Referencing requires you to exercise your **judgement**, especially when you need to document uncommon or unusual types of sources. When choosing a format, do not be afraid to adapt the formula for referencing a book, journal article, or website, depending on which is most appropriate for the source you want to cite and reference. The information below contains tips on referencing these three main types of sources and adapting the formats for less common types of sources.

REFERENCING BOOKS AND SIMILAR TYPES OF SOURCES

You usually require six pieces of information to reference a book. It can be difficult to find these six details but, with practice, you will become an expert. The tips below will help you to grow in confidence in finding and recording this information:

1 Author

2 Date

3 Title

4 Edition, if relevant

5 Place of publication

6 Publisher.

Books

Here is a book entry for the list of references with some explanation:

Give the author's surname and initial, then the date in brackets and the title in italics, followed by a full stop. Give the edition, if relevant, then the place of publication followed by a colon and the publisher

→ *Jones, P. (2010) Enhancing Academic Practice. 2nd edn. Harlow: Pearson Education*

E-books

If you are using an electronic book (e-book) or a digital format you need to add two more pieces of information. These are:

7 The full website address (URL)

8 The date of access (when you viewed the source).

The reason for giving the website address is so that readers can access the e-book for themselves. The reason for giving the date you accessed it online is that internet sites are regularly updated, so readers need to know when you viewed the book in case the interface has changed since then.

Here is an example of how to reference an e-book:

Give the author's surname and initial, then the date in brackets and the title in italics, followed by a full stop. Give the edition, if relevant, then the place of publication, followed by a colon and the publisher. Write 'available from' and give the full website address within chevrons (< >), followed by the date of access in square brackets

➤

Potter, H. (2005) *An Introduction to Human Anatomy*. 4th edn. London: Adam Arnold available from <http://anatomy/introduction/human/htm> [27th March 2006]

Authors

On a book's cover (see below) you should find the name of the authors and the title. If there is more than one author you must record the names in the order you find them written on the book cover. This is because the order may signal the amount of work each author has done, with the person who produced the most material listed first. However, most often authors are listed alphabetically and you should reproduce this order as you document their work.

INSIDE TRACK

SUCCESSFUL ACADEMIC WRITING

ANDY GILLETT, ANGELA HAMMOND & MARY MARTALA

Figure 10.4 Book authors and titles

Editors

If a book has an editor instead of an author you should write (ed.) after the name and before the date like this:

Give the editor's surname and initial, then write 'ed.' in brackets, followed by the date in brackets. Give the title in italics followed by a full stop. Give the edition, if relevant, then the place of publication followed by a colon and the publisher

→ Long, H. (ed.) (2010) *Adventures in Sound*. 2nd edn. Oxford: Oxford University Press

If a book has both an editor and an author, you should give the author first and then the date followed by the editor like this:

Give the author's surname and initial, then the date in brackets. Write 'ed. by' and give the editor's surname and initial, then the title in italics followed by a full stop. Give the edition, if relevant, then the place of publication followed by a colon and the publisher

→ Smart, K. (2010) ed. by Knowles, G. *Scholarly Writing*. 2nd edn. Oxford: Oxford University Press

Translators

If the author is the translator you should give the author as usual, then acknowledge the translator after the title like this:

Give the author's surname and initial, then the date in brackets and the title in italics, followed by a full stop. Write 'Trans. by' then give the translator's surname and initial then the place of publication followed by a colon and the publisher

→ Hatter, P. (2010) *Social Welfare*. Trans. by Hatter, P. Oxford: Oxford University Press

If the translator is not the author as well you should give the author first then the translator.

Dates of publication

Dates can be confusing, but the most important year to record is usually the date a book was first published. This is given inside the cover with all the information about the printer and publishing house. In the example below, the year to cite and reference is 2006:

First published 2006

Reprinted 2007, 2008 (twice), 2010

Dates when a book was just **reprinted** are not relevant, so in the example above you would ignore the dates after 2006. Reprinted simply means that another set of copies was made and the contents of the book remain identical, so the convention is to continue to cite the date the book was first published.

Editions

However, if the book you are using is a new or revised *edition*, you should not record the first date given, but instead record the 2nd, 3rd, or revised edition date depending which one you read. A revised edition is usually indicated on the book's cover as well as inside in the initial pages, where you will usually find information like this:

First published 2006

Second edition published 2010

When a new edition of a book is produced, the author re-writes sections and often adds material to update the publication, so the page numbers change and readers need to know which edition you have read. In the example above you would cite and reference the date as 2010, the year the second edition was published. You must also indicate this fact in your list of references entry like this:

Harrison, M. (2010) *Academic Writing: Tips and Tricks*. 2nd edn. Harlow: Pearson Education

Titles

If there is a subtitle you must include this detail in your list of references entry and add a colon before the subtitle like this:

Academic Writing: Tips and Tricks.

Capitalisation when referencing books

Always consult the guidance your tutors provide on capitalisation when referencing books. Usually in the UK, significant words in book titles are capitalised, but check the instructions in your recommended referencing style.

Note that prepositions and conjunctions are not normally capitalised.

Place of publication

The place of publication is usually a city, and this information is given inside the book cover and usually also on the title page. If you see a list of several cities you should just record the first one, so London is the place to document from this list:

> London, New York, Paris, Milan.

You may come across the full address of the publisher like this:

> Edinburgh Gate
> Harlow
> Essex CM20 2JE
> England.

In this case you need to identify the city, which is Harlow in the example above. Essex is a county and England is a country, so you do not document these in your list of references.

Publisher

The publisher is relatively easy to identify because there is usually a logo or indication of who published a book on the front cover, and often on the spine of the book. The publisher is usually written inside the book cover in the initial pages, for example, like this:

> Pearson Education Limited.

In the example above you would not include the word 'Limited' but simply write 'Pearson Education' as the publisher.

So, if you put all five pieces of information together, your entry in the list of references for a book should be as shown in Table 10.1.

Table 10.1 Books

Author's surname and initial	Date	Book title	Edition	Place of publication	Publisher
Jones, B.	(2010)	*Academic Writing: Tips and Tricks.*	2nd edn.	Harlow:	Pearson Education

Other types of books

Edited collections

Edited collections are books containing chapters written by different authors. You will usually need to cite material from a specific chapter, so record the name of the chapter author, the chapter title, and the first and last page numbers for the chapter. In addition, document the same information you usually need to reference a book.

Here is an example of how to reference a chapter:

<table>
<tr>
<td>Give the surname and initial of the chapter author, then the date in brackets and the chapter title followed by a full stop. Write 'In', then the title of the edited collection in italics, followed by a full stop. Write 'Ed. by' then the editor's surname and initial followed by the place of publication followed by a colon and the publisher, then a colon and the page numbers of the article   ⟶</td>
<td>Skillen, J. (2006) Teaching Academic Writing from the 'Centre' in Australian Universities. In Teaching Academic Writing in UK Higher Education: Theories, Practices and Models. Ed. by Ganobcsik-Williams, L. Houndmills: Palgrave Macmillan: 140–53</td>
</tr>
</table>

A note about referencing chapters in edited collections

Some referencing styles instruct you to put single quote marks around chapter titles. Follow your recommended guidelines and if unsure, check with your tutor.

So, your entry in the list of references for a chapter from an edited collection should be as shown in Table 10.2.

Table 10.2 Edited collections

Author's surname and initial	Date	Chapter title	Write 'In' then the title of the edited collection	Edition	Write 'Ed. by' then the editor's surname and initial	Place	Publisher	Page numbers of chapter
Skillen, J.	(2006)	Teaching Academic Writing from the 'Centre' in Australian Universities.	In *Teaching Academic Writing in UK Higher Education: Theories, Practices and Models.*		Ed. by Ganobcsik-Williams, L.	Houndmills:	Palgrave Macmillan:	140–53

Reports

The formula for referencing reports is similar to the method for referencing books. Here is an example of how to reference a report:

Give the author or corporate author and the date in brackets, then the title in italics followed by the number of the report and a full stop. Give the place the report was produced, and a colon, then the organisation or publisher

Dietetics Committee (2009) Department of Health Report on Dietary Health no. 41. London: Stationery Office

Pamphlets

The formula for referencing pamphlets, leaflets, and brochures is similar to the method for referencing books. Here is an example of how to reference a pamphlet:

Give the author or corporate author and the date in brackets, then the title in italics, followed by a full stop. Give the place the pamphlet was produced, and a colon, then the organisation or publisher

National Health Service (2009) Catch it, Bin it, Kill it. Coventry: University Hospital

Unpublished booklets, manuals, guides, and handbooks

The formula for referencing any unpublished source is similar to the method for referencing books. Here is an example of how to reference an unpublished booklet:

Give the author and the date in brackets, then the title, followed by a full stop. Give the place the source was produced, and a colon, then the organisation

Dawson, E. (2010) Guide to Writing Reports. Coventry: Coventry University

REFERENCING SECONDARY SOURCES

Secondary sources are sources cited in materials you have read, but you have not seen them yourself. To reference a secondary source, give the publication details for the secondary source, followed by the publication details for the source that you have read.

Here is an example of how to reference a secondary source:

For the secondary source, give the author's surname and initial, then the date in brackets and the title in italics, followed by a full stop. Give the place of publication followed by a colon and the publisher then a full stop. Write 'Cited in' then do the same for the source you have read

Adams, K. (2007) Researching and Writing. Harlow: Pearson Education. Cited in Downs, E. (2010) Strategies for Success. Harlow: Pearson Education

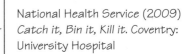

REFERENCING JOURNAL ARTICLES AND SIMILAR TYPES OF SOURCES

Journal articles

You usually need seven pieces of information to reference a journal article. These are:

1 Author

2 Date

3 Article title

4 Journal title

5 Volume number

6 Part or issue number (if there is one)

7 Page numbers of the article.

Here is an example with more information about the formula for referencing a journal article:

Give the author's surname and initial, the date in brackets, and the title of the article followed by a full stop. Give the title of the journal in italics, the volume number, the part (or issue) number in brackets, then the page numbers of the article

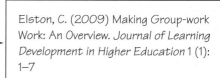

Elston, C. (2009) Making Group-work Work: An Overview. *Journal of Learning Development in Higher Education* 1 (1): 1–7

A note about referencing articles in journals

Some referencing styles instruct you to put single quote marks around article titles. Follow your recommended guidelines and if unsure, check with your tutor.

Accessing journal articles online

If you download an online journal article and your version is exactly the same as the hard copy in the journal, including the page numbers, you should reference the article as if you were using the hard copy. However, if the page numbers in your version are not the same as the hard copy in the journal you need to add two pieces of information. These are:

■ The full website address (URL)

■ The date of access.

Here is an example of how to reference an article you have accessed online when the page numbers are different to the hard copy in the journal:

If you are supplying the URL, write 'available from' and give the full website address within chevrons (< >), followed by the date of access in square brackets ➙

> Elston, C. (2009) Making Group-work Work: An Overview. *Journal of Learning Development in Higher Education* 1 (1): 1–8 available from <http://www.aldinhe. ac.uk/ojs/index.php?journal=jldhe& page=article&op=view&path%5B%5D= 36&path%5B%5D=17> [1st October 2009]

So, your entry in the list of references for a journal article you have accessed online should be as shown in Table 10.3:

Table 10.3 Journal articles

Author's surname and initial	Date	Article title	Journal title	Volume no.	Part or issue no.	Page numbers of article	Full website address (URL)	Date of access
Elston, C.	(2009)	Making Group-work Work: An Overview.	Journal of Learning Development in Higher Education	1	(1):	1–8	available from <http://www. aldinhe.ac. uk/ojs/index. php?journal= jldhe&page= article&op= view&path%5 B%5D= 36&path% 5B%5D=17>	[1st October 2009]

Newspapers and magazines

The formula for referencing articles in newspapers and magazines is similar to the method for referencing journal articles, and if you access a newspaper online you should include the website address in the same way. Here is an example of how to reference a newspaper article you have accessed online:

Give the surname and initials of the authors, the date in brackets, and the title of the article followed by a full stop

Give the name of the newspaper in italics, then the day it was printed. If you are supplying the URL, write 'available from' and give the full website address within chevrons (< >) followed by the date of access in square brackets

> Clark, D., O'Connor, M., Bangay, R. and Roche, R. (2009) Guardian's Quick Carbon Calculator. *Guardian* 21st October 2009, available from <http://www.guardian.co.uk/environment/ interactive/2009/oct/20/guardian- quick-carbon-calculator> [25th October 2009]

A note about referencing articles

Some referencing styles instruct you to put single quote marks around article titles. Follow your recommended guidelines and if unsure, check with your tutor.

REFERENCING WEBSITES AND SIMILAR TYPES OF SOURCES

You usually need five pieces of information to reference a journal article. These are:

1 Author

2 Date

3 Webpage title

4 The full website address (URL)

5 The date of access.

Here is an example of how to reference a website:

Give the author or corporate author, the date in brackets, then the title of the webpage in italics. Write 'available from' and give the full website address within chevrons (< >) followed by the date of access in square brackets

→ Economics Network (2009) *Effective Writing and Referencing* available from <http://studyingeconomics.ac.uk/effective-writing/> [1st October 2009]

So, your entry for the list of references for a website should be as shown in Table 10.4:

Table 10.4 Websites

Corporate author	Date	Webpage title	Full website address (URL)	Date of access
Economics Network	(2009)	*Effective Writing and Referencing*	available from <http://studyingeconomics. ac.uk/effective-writing/>	[1st October 2009]

Audiovisual recordings as downloads

Downloaded sources are referenced in a similar way to a website. As there is such a range of different digital sources, the best advice to give is that you should adapt the formula for referencing websites using your own judgement, and as long as you are clear and consistent you will do a good job. If you have any concerns about referencing more unusual digital sources, ask your tutor for advice or seek guidance at your university library. Here is an example of how to reference a downloaded audio source:

Give the corporate author, the date in brackets, then the title of the download in italics followed by a full stop, then the day and time it was broadcast. Write 'available from' and give the full website address within chevrons (< >) followed by the date of access in square brackets

➡

BBC Radio 4 (2009) *St Thomas Aquinas. In Our Time with Melvyn Bragg*. 17th September 2009 9.00am, available from <http://www.bbc.co.uk/podcasts/series/iot> [23rd September 2009]

Audiovisual recordings (not downloaded)

Give the same author as you gave in your in-text citations and supply enough information for readers to find the source for themselves. Here is an example of how to reference a DVD giving the director as the author:

Give the surname and initial of the author, the date in brackets, then the title of the DVD in italics followed a full stop. Give the name of the company who produced the DVD

➡

Minghella, A. (2004) *Cold Mountain*. Buena Vista Home Entertainment

Blogs

The formula for referencing blogs is similar to the method for referencing websites. Here is an example:

Give the surname and initial of the author, the date in brackets, then the title of the entry in italics, followed by a full stop, then the day and time it was added. Write 'available from' and give the full website address within chevrons (< >) followed by the date of access in square brackets

➡

Dwyer, J. (2009) *Back to School: Tips for Teachers*. 18th September 2009 8.01pm available from <http://blog.facebook.com/> [22nd September 2009]

Online discussion fora and mailing lists

The formula for referencing discussion lists is similar to the method for referencing websites. Here is an example:

Give the surname and initial of the author, the date in brackets, then the title of the discussion thread in italics, followed by a full stop, then the day and time the comment was added. Write 'available from' and give the full website address within chevrons (< >) followed by the date of access in square brackets

➡

Harris, O. (2009) *Teaching Practice*. 1st September 2009 5.30pm available from <eataw-conf@lists.hum.ku.dk> [22nd September 2009]

Personal communications

The formula for referencing personal communications is similar to the method for referencing websites. Here is an example of how to reference an email:

Give the surname and initial of the author, the date in brackets, then the subject of the email in italics, followed by a full stop, then the day and time it was added. Write 'available from' and give the full website address within chevrons (< >) followed by the date of access in square brackets

→

Simms, P. (2010) *Enquiry re Invoice.* 5th January 2010 1.10pm available from <http://mail.live.com/default.aspx?&n=1011776457> [10th January 2010]

Lectures

The formula for referencing lectures is similar to the method for referencing a website, especially if you downloaded notes from your module web.

Should you borrow material from lectures?

It is not necessarily appropriate to cite and reference lectures in your academic writing because lecturers usually expect you to conduct independent research based on the ideas they share and the reading lists they distribute at lectures.

Here is an example of how to reference a lecture:

Give the surname and initial of the lecturer as author, the date in brackets, then the title of the lecture in italics followed by a full stop. Give the course code, a comma, then the day the lecture was delivered. Add a full stop then the university. Write 'available from' and give the full website address within chevrons (< >), followed by the date of access in square brackets (omit the URL and date of access if you did not download the lecture notes)

→

Hobbs, R. (2010) *Case Law and Legal Writing.* Module 102 Law, 10th February 2010. Coventry University available from <http://legalwriting.ac.uk/caselaw-module102/> [1st February 2010]

Decisions about referencing

This section of Chapter 10 has explained how to reference using the Harvard style. It has covered the main points you need to know and recommended that you seek advice from your tutors or library specialists when you are unsure about any aspect of citing and referencing. It has indicated that there are times when you have to make decisions about how to reference sources. Base these decisions on the three following rules:

1 Be *clear* about where you have accessed sources

2 Be *consistent* in documenting sources in your list of references

3 Be *comprehensive* in giving all the details readers require to find sources for themselves.

SUMMARY

This chapter has explained how to use the Harvard style and has provided a wide range of examples (Deane 2009b). It has stressed the need to be clear and consistent as you acknowledge all the sources you use in your academic writing. It has emphasised that as you cite and reference unusual sources you need to use your own judgement and make decisions based on the advice of your tutors, library specialists, and your recommended referencing guidelines.

The main arguments in this chapter:

■ To cite sources you should give the author, date, and page number when appropriate

■ To reference sources you should learn the format for each type of source in your recommended referencing guidelines.

11 ACADEMIC DISCIPLINES AND REFERENCING SYSTEMS

This chapter introduces three commonly used referencing styles and their disciplinary contexts. It points out that although the terminology associated with each referencing style is different, you always need to master the two elements of acknowledging sources in-text and acknowledging sources in full at the end of your writing (Williams and Carroll 2009: 7). You need to check which style you should use before you begin your research, writing, and referencing.

The chapter covers:

- Referencing styles used in the humanities
- Referencing styles used in the social sciences
- Referencing styles used in the life and physical sciences.

Using this chapter

Topic	Page
Similarities between referencing styles	138
Humanities: Modern Language Association (MLA)	138
Social sciences: American Psychological Association (APA)	139
Life and physical sciences: Council of Science Editors (CSE)	140

INTRODUCTION

Following the detailed exploration of the Harvard style in Chapter 10, Chapter 11 offers a brief introduction to alternative referencing systems and outlines the disciplines in which they are used. Remember to **check with your tutors** which style you should use and ask their advice if you are unsure about any aspect of citing and referencing.

SIMILARITIES BETWEEN REFERENCING STYLES

The two main categories of referencing systems are numerical styles (which require the insertion of footnotes or endnotes) and parenthetical styles (which require the use of brackets).

Although this chapter gives examples of different referencing styles it emphasises the similarities between them, and you will notice that the variations are mostly a matter of the order for formatting details and the use of punctuation. Therefore once you have a good understanding of the rationale and conventions for one referencing style, it will be easy for you to master the use of other systems. For this reason, *Academic Research, Writing and Referencing* dedicates Chapter 10 to explaining one style in detail.

It is beyond the scope of this book to offer in-depth guidance on many different referencing styles and this would be inappropriate because, unlike for the Harvard style, there are official publications for most other referencing styles providing explanations, examples, and extensive advice on their use within disciplinary contexts.

Remember that whichever referencing style you use there are two elements you need to master (Williams and Carroll 2009: 7):

1 In-text acknowledgements of sources

2 A list of acknowledged sources in full at the end of your writing.

The terms for these two elements vary, and you will need to familiarise yourself with the terminology of your chosen referencing style.

HUMANITIES

Modern Language Association (MLA) style

The Modern Language Association (MLA) style is a parenthetical style for citing and referencing sources, which is used in English studies and other humanities subjects.

MLA in-text citations

To use the MLA style either refer to authors directly or cite them in brackets. Also give the page number:

> In *The Bell Jar* **Plath** explores a young woman's experiences of mental illness, which end in a thought-provoking way **(234)**.

MLA list of works cited

Each in-text citation in the MLA style must be followed up with an entry in the list of works cited like this:

> Plath, Sylvia. *The Bell Jar*. rev. edn. London: Faber and Faber, 1963. Print.

For comprehensive information and examples of how to cite and reference in the MLA style, see:

Modern Language Association. *MLA Handbook for Writers of Research Papers*. 7th ed. New York: Modern Language Association of America, 2009. Print.

Modern Language Association. *MLA Style Manual and Guide to Scholarly Publishing*. 3rd ed. New York: Modern Language Association of America, 2008. Print.

SOCIAL SCIENCES

American Psychological Association (APA) style

The American Psychological Association (APA) style is a parenthetical style for citing and referencing, which is used in psychology and other social science subjects.

APA in-text citations

To use the APA style, either refer to authors directly or cite them in brackets. Also give the date and page number:

> In *The Bell Jar* **Plath (1963)** explores a young woman's experiences of mental illness, which end in a thought-provoking way **(p. 234)**.

APA references

Each in-text citation in the APA style must be followed up with an entry in the list of references like this:

Plath, S. (1963) *The Bell Jar*. rev. edn. London: Faber and Faber.

For comprehensive information and examples of how to cite and reference in the APA style, see:

American Psychological Association. (2009). *Publication Manual of the American Psychological Association* (6th edn). Washington: American Psychological Association.

SCIENCES

Council of Science Editors (CSE) style

The Council of Science Editors (CSE) style permits use of a numerical style for citing and referencing sources, which is used in life and physical sciences.

CSE superscript citations

To use the CSE style you can choose either parentheses or superscript citation, but you must not mix the two methods. For superscript citation, insert an endnote and give full details in the cited references list.

In *The Bell Jar* **Plath** explores a young woman's experiences of mental illness, which end in a thought-provoking way.[1]

CSE cited references

Each superscript citation in the CSE style must be followed up with an entry in the cited references list like this:

1. Plath, S. *The Bell Jar*. London: Faber and Faber; 1963.

For comprehensive information and examples of how to cite and reference in the CSE style see:

Council of Science Editors. *Scientific style and format: The CSE manual for authors, editors, and publishers*. 7th edn. Reston (VA): The Council of Science Editors; 2006.

SUMMARY

This chapter has introduced three commonly used referencing systems and their disciplinary contexts. It has pointed out that although the terminology associated with each style differs, you always need to master the two elements of citing in-text and listing your sources in full. The chapter has reiterated that you must check with your tutors which style to use before you begin your research, writing, and referencing.

The main arguments in this chapter:

- Find out which referencing style is recommended by your tutors
- Learn the terminology and conventions associated with this style
- Consult the official publication on your recommended style, if relevant.

CONCLUSION:
SUCCEEDING IN THE ACADEMY

The aim of this book is to foster your confidence in undertaking research, writing, and referencing at an advanced level. It has sought to equip you to be an organised and independent scholar by adopting a proactive approach tailored to your strengths and subject of study.

Part 1 introduced the culture of scholarly practice and pointed out that your academic success is in your own hands. By explaining academic integrity and ways of avoiding plagiarism, it suggested ways of managing information, planning your time, and keeping complete records of your sources.

Part 2 outlined the LARC research strategy, which stands for Locating, Assessing, and Reading Critically. Although these three stages of research were presented in a linear way, you should move back and forth between the stages as you select, reject, and evaluate sources. By suggesting how to be savvy in your use of sources, this part reminded you to start research early, respect your deadline, and keep your purpose for writing in sight.

Part 3 demonstrated how to integrate sources into your writing by quoting, paraphrasing, summarising, and critiquing while acknowledging sources in a scholarly way. It explained that these techniques should all be used in your academic writing to display agility and critical thinking as you draw upon research. It emphasised that all writing is indebted to existing ideas and that evaluating scholarship can help you contribute to knowledge.

Part 4 explored how to cite and reference in the Harvard style and discussed other citing and referencing systems because the conventions are distinctive in each discipline. It explained that you need to check the recommended referencing style in your subject area and seek your tutors' advice. It emphasised the need to learn the conventions for citing and referencing in your field and practising until they become automatic.

In summary, the most important point in *Academic Research, Writing and Referencing* is that effective time management can help you avoid plagiarism, enjoy writing, and feel confident about referencing. You will develop your own strategies for using time efficiently depending on your preferences and commitments, but the purpose of this book has been to provide you with some tools with which to experiment until you establish the routine and methods which work best for you.

GLOSSARY

Abbreviation An abbreviation is the shortened form of a word or phrase. The first time you use a term you should write it in full, but for later instances within a single document you can abbreviate.

Academic paper An academic paper is an assignment, article, or other document that is written for an academic audience. A paper may be written as part of an assessment for an undergraduate or a postgraduate degree, produced for publication in a journal, or delivered at a conference (Deane 2009a: 3).

Acronym An acronym is a word formed from the first letters of a name or phrase. The first time you use a term you should write it in full, but for later instances in a single document you can use an acronym.

Appendix An appendix contains extra information that is not directly necessary for a document, but which provides supplementary details. In a long document such as a dissertation, thesis, or report, writers include an appendix at the end. A document may contain more than one appendix, and the plural form is appendices. Appendices should be labelled 1, 2, etc. for clarity.

Bibliography A bibliography is a list of all the sources you have read in preparation for writing a document. This is different to a list of references, which gives full information solely for the sources acknowledged in your in-text citations.

Blog Blog is short for 'weblog'. It is a type of website, often in the format of a diary in reverse order (starting with the latest entry). On the internet, blog entries can be shared in the public domain. Blog entries must be cited and referenced.

Browser A browser is a software tool that enables users to view or search for information available on the internet; for instance, Internet Explorer™ is a browser. A browser is used to navigate the web and to view information on webpages.

Circa (c.) c. is used to estimate a date; for instance, c.1100. This term is an abbreviation of the Latin word 'circa' which means about or approximately. Being an abbreviation, you should add a full stop at the end to indicate missing letters.

Cite To cite means to refer to a source in the main body of a document. Whenever you cite a source in the main body of your document, you must also give full publication or internet details in the list of references in accordance with the instructions in your chosen referencing style.

Collusion Collusion is working secretly with another person to produce a piece of work that you later present as your own without crediting the other person. Collusion can also involve copying from another person or asking someone to produce work for you. Collusion is different from collaborating legitimately with colleagues, which is a normal and fruitful part of academic life.

Corporate author A corporate author is an organisation or corporate body that produces a source. A corporate author could be a government organisation such as the Department of Health (DoH), and websites are often produced by a corporate author.

Database A database is an electronic collection of data stored in a software programme to organise and retrieve data. You can access the best range of up-to-date sources by using a database in your subject area.

Date of access When citing and referencing a source you have accessed online it is important to give the date you accessed the source in accordance with the instructions in your chosen referencing style.

E-book An e-book is a book that is available electronically. If the page numbers are the same as the hard copy (for instance because the book is accessible in PDF) you should cite and reference the book as normal. If you access a source online and the page numbers are not stable or you think readers would benefit from knowing where to access the source online, you should give the web address and date of access in your list of references entry.

Et al. et al. is an abbreviation of the Latin term 'et alii' which means 'and the others'. Being an abbreviation you should add a full stop at the end to indicate missing letters. You should use et al. in accordance with your chosen referencing style to indicate multiple authors. Note that when using et al. in your in-text citations you should usually give the full list of authors' names in your list of references to credit the intellectual property of each contributor.

Figure When you borrow a visual source you must label it as a figure and write a caption for it. Then make a list of figures and put it in the contents page at the start of your document.

Ibid. ibid. is an abbreviation of the Latin term 'ibidem' which means 'in the same place'. Being an abbreviation you should add a full stop at the end to indicate missing letters. In some referencing styles ibid. is used to indicate that information about a source is repeated. Follow the guidance in your chosen referencing style.

Image An image must be cited and referenced when borrowed from a source and used in your writing.

Intellectual honesty Clear referencing enables you to display intellectual honesty about where you have borrowed information from (Deane 2009a: 5).

Intellectual property You must cite and reference every idea, image, statistic, etc. you borrow from a source because it is the intellectual property of the individual or groups of people who produced it. Legally, ideas belong to the person or people who originally expressed them, and if you borrow ideas you must credit the owner (Deane 2009a: 5).

Internet The internet is much bigger than individual websites. It is the technical infrastructure that includes websites and webpages which are interlinked over a worldwide area network.

In-text citation An in-text citation is used to signal the use of a source in the main body of a document when you borrow ideas, images, statistics, etc. Every time you give an in-text citation you must ensure that you have given full publication details in the list of references at the end of your document. Follow the guidance in your chosen referencing style.

Glossary

Issue number (or part number) Most academic journals are issued multiple times in a year. Many are issued every season, so there is a spring, summer, autumn, and winter issue. These are numbered 1, 2, 3, 4, etc. When you reference a journal article you should identify the issue or part number.

List of references A list of references gives full publication or internet details for all the in-text citations in your document. This list goes on a separate page at the end of your work and the entries should be ordered alphabetically according to the author's surname or the corporate author. Follow the guidance in your chosen referencing style.

Numerical data Numerical data, including statistics and other data, must be cited and referenced when borrowed from a source and used in your writing.

Online journal article An online journal article is a digital version of an article. If the page numbers are the same as the hard copy in the journal (for instance because the article is accessible in PDF) you should cite and reference it as usual. If you access a source online and the page numbers are not stable or you think readers would benefit from knowing where to access the source online, you should give the web address and date of access.

Op. cit. op. cit. is an abbreviation of the Latin term 'opere citato' which means 'in the work cited'. Being an abbreviation you should add a full stop at the end of each of the two words to indicate missing letters. In some referencing styles op. cit. is used after the author's name to refer again to the work previously cited. Follow the guidance in your chosen referencing style.

Paraphrase Paraphrasing is a way of integrating sources into your writing. To para-phrase a source means to put it into your own words in an accurate way, so be careful not to distort the meaning as you rephrase the words. When you paraphrase a source you must cite and reference it, and you should usually introduce the source and evaluate it if appropriate. A paraphrase of a source should be approximately the same length as the original passage. Paraphrasing is a useful method of integrating research into your writing because it shows that you have understood the source.

PDF A PDF is a stable way of saving and sharing sources. This term is an acronym for 'portable document format'. A PDF is useful for citing and referencing sources you have accessed online because the page numbers do not usually change from the original printed source.

Plagiarism Plagiarism is the omission of acknowledgements for your sources, or the attempt to present the intellectual property of another person as your own. The two main categories of plagiarism are intentional and unintentional, and there are serious penalties for both kinds. A distinction is not necessarily made between the two categories of plagia-rism because students are responsible for adopting scholarly practice and are expected to produce their own work in order to gain qualifications.

Quote Quoting is a way of integrating sources into your writing. To quote a source means to repeat exactly the words used by a writer or speaker, and this term is short for quotation. Always give the page number when you quote a source so your readers can locate the exact passage. When you quote a source you must cite and reference it, and you should put the quote in quotation marks according to the instructions in your chosen referencing style. You should introduce the source and evaluate it to demonstrate your critical thinking skills. Quoting should be balanced with paraphrasing, summarising, and critiquing sources because quoting does not necessarily demonstrate your understanding of a source.

Quoting a long passage If you are quoting more than approximately 20 words you should separate the quote from your own writing and indent it. You should introduce the source and evaluate it to demonstrate your critical thinking skills. When you quote a source you must cite and reference it, and give the page number so your readers can locate the exact passage. If you are using a short quote that you wish to emphasise you can also indent this (if it can stand alone and make sense to the reader).

Reference A reference is an entry in the list of references at the end of a document that gives the full publication or internet details for a source. Each in-text citation must be followed up with an entry in the reference list so readers can easily locate the sources you have used. Follow the guidance in your chosen referencing style.

Search engine A search engine is a device that enables you to search for information on the internet. There are many popular search engines, but beware of commercial search engines because they will not necessarily give you scholarly results.

Secondary sources Secondary sources are sources you have not read yourself, which are cited and referenced in a source you have read. It is preferable to locate the original source and cite it as usual if you can because this demonstrates your research skills. If you are unable to locate a secondary source, you should make it clear to readers that you are citing and referencing a source you have not read yourself, and you should give the page number of the source you have read so readers can easily locate the passage.

Signal phrase A signal phrase is used to signal the integration of a source into your document. Using signal phrases is a useful way to introduce sources you quote, paraphrase, summarise, and critique sources in your writing.

Spoken source A spoken source is any source that was not originally written down, including a recording of an interview, conversation, performance, etc. All spoken sources must be cited and referenced. Follow the guidance in your chosen referencing style.

Summary Summarising is a way of integrating sources into your writing. To summarise a source means to give a brief account of the main points or arguments. When you summarise a source you must cite and reference it. A summary of a source is usually much shorter than the original passage. Summarising is an effective means of integrating research into your writing because it shows that you have fully understood the source and that you can make this information work for you.

Table When you borrow data, statistics, or other numerical information from a source you should usually label it as a table and write a caption for it. Then make a list of tables and include it in the contents page at the beginning of your document.

URL A URL is a web address; it is an acronym for 'uniform resource locator'. It is used to locate an address on the internet that is shown in the bar at the top of any webpage you view.

Visual source A visual source is any source that is predominantly an image rather than text. This may be a photograph, painting, sculpture, graphics, etc. All visual sources must be cited and referenced. Follow the guidance in your chosen referencing style.

Website A website is a collection of webpages. A webpage is a single element within a website that incorporates information, and is usually linked to other webpages.

QUIZ ANSWERS

Chapter 1

Unlike Example 7, example 2 demonstrates academic integrity most effectively because the intellectual property of each scholar is acknowledged in a transparent way. Points made by Kendall are attributed to her, while the argument advanced by Harris that students sometimes misunderstand assignment briefs is credited to that author. The writer provides an in-text citation acknowledging the secondary source written by Harris that is cited in Kendall's argument. For more information about citing secondary sources see Chapter 10.

Chapter 2

1 There are no missing in-text citations. Notice that the authors do not cite the references to well known dates and events because this constitutes general knowledge in the fields of business and politics. Scholars working in this area also know the remit and history of organisations such as the World Bank and the International Monetary Fund, so these do not need to be cited.

2 In Example 1 the writer has taken this photograph herself and made this clear to her readers, so it is not necessary to provide an in-text citation in this instance, as she has not borrowed it from a source.

3 In Example 2 the writer is stating a well known fact that is general knowledge and not the intellectual property of Edwards (2010), so it is not necessary to provide an in-text citation in this instance.

4 In Example 3 the writer is referring to a well-known story, so it is not necessary to provide an in-text citation in this instance. (If the writer was discussing the Grimm version of Cinderella it would be appropriate to cite that source.)

5 In Example 4 the writer is referring to the scholars' intellectual property, so it is necessary to provide an in-text citation for the sources in this instance.

Chapter 3

1 A wide range of scholarly sources is readily available via your university library catalogue.

2 Relevance, ready availability, and reliability of source materials.

3 Peer review ensures the quality of academic literature.

4 Start by searching for general sources to give you a grounding in the subject area.

5 A monograph is a book based on a research project or doctoral thesis. Monographs are useful in providing information about a specific topic because they explore issues and arguments in depth.

Chapter 4

1 Thesis. This word is short for hypothesis and it means the main argument of a source. You must be clear about a source's main argument before you select it for use in your academic writing.

2 If appropriate, you can critique the use of evidence in a source to demonstrate your own critical thinking.

3 Yes. It is inevitable that when you assess the relevance of sources you will find that some are not suitable for your purpose owing to the content, style, or intended audience, for instance.

4 The index lists key words and subjects discussed in a source and it gives you quick access to relevant passages, which you can read to test whether the text is appropriate and informative.

5 An abstract is a synopsis of a source's scope, argument, and methodology. Abstracts provide concise information to help you judge whether to read more of a source.

Chapter 5

1 The main topic of this extract is indicated by the subheading: 'A role identity perspective on vocational indecision'.

2 Two. The in-text citations used to support the authors' referral to role identity theory are Stryker (1980) and Tajfel and Turner (1985). They date from the 1980s.

3 Salient role identities have the greatest meaning to a person according to Ng and Feldman (2009).

4 To support the point that for many students the two most salient life roles are student and worker, Ng and Feldman cite Super (1990).

5 The article by Ng and Feldman (2009) focuses on the two identities of student and worker.

Chapter 6

1 Example 1 is well cited. However, the writer could change the capital A to lower case and indicate this with square brackets like this: '[a]ntidepressant prescribing...'

2 Example 2 is almost accurate. The writer should indent this longer passage and separate it from his or her own writing. Passages longer than approximately 20 words should usually be separated and indented, but you should follow the guidelines in your chosen referencing style.

3 Example 3 is inaccurate because the writer has placed the second quotation mark in the middle of the borrowed material rather than at the end. This error constitutes plagiarism because, by failing to signal all of the quoted text, the writer is claiming credit for intellectual property that belongs to Moore et al. (2009).

4 Example 4 is inaccurate because the writer has not used quotation marks to signal the borrowed text. This error constitutes plagiarism because, by failing to signal quotations from the article explicitly, the writer is claiming credit for intellectual property that belongs to Moore *et al.* (2009). Italics are not usually appropriate for quotations, but you should follow the guidelines in your chosen referencing style. In addition, the writer has omitted to give the page number in the in-text citation.

5 Example 5 is technically accurate but this is not a good example of scholarly practice because the writer has failed to introduce the quotation or comment on it. Always integrate quotes into your own writing by explaining the relevance of applications for your discussion. As in Example 2, the writer should indent a longer quote.

Chapter 7

1 Example 1 is an accurate paraphrase and in-text citation. The writer has understood the meaning of this passage in the wider context of Marsh's article and has worked hard to capture the sense. This paraphrase is accurately cited with the author, the date, and the page number given.

2 Example 2 is an inaccurate paraphrase. The writer has kept too much of the text in Marsh's exact words and this paraphrase is not cited properly. There is no indication of the author's name or the date of publication. This constitutes plagiarism because the author is not acknowledged.

3 Although the paraphrase is accurate, it is not cited properly because there is no indication of the date of publication or the page number.

4 Example 4 is inaccurate because the writer has not cited Marsh. This error constitutes plagiarism because, by failing to signal that the passage is a paraphrase of Marsh (2004), the writer is claiming credit for his intellectual property.

5 Example 5 is an inaccurate paraphrase because the writer has not put the exact passage from Marsh's article into her own words. Although a clear citation is given, this is an example of a summary because it is so concise.

Chapter 8

1 Example 1 is an accurate summary and citation. As this summary is taken from a specific page the writer has included the page number. The writer has given a concise version of relevant points in this passage and has acknowledged both Howard (2007) and Trimbur (2000) appropriately. For guidance on citing sources mentioned in texts (known as secondary sources), see Chapter 10.

2 Example 2 is an inaccurate citation. Although the writer has written an effective, concise version of Howard's point, this is not cited properly as no date is given for the source.

3 Example 3 is an accurate summary because the writer has captured a relevant point efficiently and given a full citation. As this summary is taken from a specific page the writer has included the page number.

4 Example 4 is an inaccurate citation because the writer has not acknowledged the article by Howard (2007) but instead has credited Trimbur (2000), whose work she has not read. In addition, no date is given for the source by Trimbur. This constitutes plagiarism because Howard is not acknowledged.

5 Example 5 is inaccurate because the writer has not cited Howard. This error constitutes plagiarism because, by failing to acknowledge Howard (2007), the writer is claiming credit for her intellectual property.

LIST OF REFERENCES

American Psychological Association (2009) *Publication Manual of the American Psychological Association.* 6th edn. Washington: American Psychological Association

Barnet, S. and Bedau, H. (2008) *From Critical Thinking to Argument: A Portable Guide.* Boston: Bedford/St Martin's

BBC Radio 4 (2009) *St Thomas Aquinas. In Our Time with Melvyn Bragg.* 17th September 2009 9.00am available from http://www.bbc.co.uk/podcasts/series/iot [23rd September 2009]

Council of Science Editors (2006) *Scientific Style and Format: The CSE Manual for Authors. Editors, and Publishers.* 7th edn. Reston: The Council of Science Editors

Deane, M. (2009a) Coventry University Harvard Reference Style Glossary. 3rd edn. Coventry: Coventry University

Deane, M. (2009b) Coventry University Harvard Reference Style Guide. 3rd edn. Coventry: Coventry University

DeSena, L. H. (2007) *Preventing Plagiarism: Tips and Techniques.* Urbana: National Council of Teachers of English

DeVoss, D. and Rosati, A. C. (2002) 'It Wasn't Me, Was It?' Plagiarism and the Web. *Computers and Composition* 19 (2): 191–203

Dwyer, J. (2009) *Back to School: Tips for Teachers.* 18th September 2009 8.01pm available from http://blog.facebook.com/ [22nd September 2009]

Economics Network (2009) *Effective Writing and Referencing* available from http://studyingeconomics.ac.uk/effective-writing/ [1st October 2009]

Foster, S. (2009) *How to Write Better Law Essays: Tools and Techniques for Success in Exams and Assignments.* 2nd edn. Harlow: Pearson Longman

Gornall, J. (2009) Whistleblowing: The Price of Silence. *British Medical Journal* 339 (7728): 1000–4 available from <http://www.bmj.com/content/vol339/issue7728/> [1st November 2009]

Hacker, D. (2006) *Research and Documentation in the Electronic Age.* 4th edn. Boston: Bedford/St Martin's

Harris, O. (2009) *Teaching Practice.* 1st September 2009 5.30pm available from <eataw-conf 2 lists.hum.ku.dk>[22nd September 2009]

Howard, R. M. (2007) Understanding 'Internet Plagiarism'. *Computers and Composition* 24: 3–15 (p. 11)

List of References

Kendall, A. (2008) The Assignment Sheet Mystery. *The Writing Lab Newsletter* 33 (1): 1–5 available from <http://writinglabnewsletter.org/archives/v33/33.1.pdf> [5th September 2009]

Lawson, T. C., Lindeque, J. P. and McGuire, S. M. (2009) Multilateralism and the Multinational Enterprise. *Business and Politics* 11 (2): 1–26

Lunsford, A.A. (2008) *The St martin's Handbook*. 6th edn. Boston: Bedford/St Martin's

Lunsford, A. A. (2009) *The Everyday Writer.* 4th edn. Boston: Bedford/St Martin's

Marsh, B. (2004) Turnitin.com and the Scriptural Enterprise of Plagiarism Detection. *Computers and Composition* 21: 427–38

Minghella, A. (2004) *Cold Mountain*. Buena Vista Home Entertainment

Modern Language Association (2008) *MLA Style Manual and Guide to Scholarly Publishing*. 3rd edn. New York: Modern Language Association of America

Modern Language Association (2009) *MLA Handbook for Writers of Research Papers*. 7th edn. New York: Modern Language Association of America

Moore, M., Yuen, H. M., Dunn, N., Mullee, M., Maskell, J. and Kendrick, T. (2009) Explaining the Rise in Antidepressant Prescribing: A Descriptive Study Using the General Practice Research Database. *British Medical Journal* 339 (7727) available from <http://www.bmj.com/cgi/reprint/339/oct15_2/b3999> [1st November 2009]

Neville, C. (2007) *The Complete Guide to Referencing and Avoiding Plagiarism*. Maidenhead: Open University Press

Ng, T. W. H. and Feldman, D. C. (2009) Personality, Social Relationships, and Vocational Indecision Among College Students: The Mediating Effects of Identity Construction. *Career Development International* 14 (4): 309–32

Plath, S. (1963) *The Bell Jar*. London: Faber and Faber

Sorapure, M., Inglesby, P. and Yatchisin, G. (1998) Web Literacy: Challenges and Opportunities for Research in a New Medium. *Computers and Composition* 15: 409–24

Williams, K. and Carroll, J. (2009) *Referencing and Understanding Plagiarism*. Houndmills: Palgrave Macmillan

BIBLIOGRAPHY

Clark, D., O'Connor, M., Bangay, R. and Roche, R. (2009) The Guardian's Quick Carbon Calculator. *Guardian* 21st October 2009 available from http://www.guardian.co.uk/environment/interactive/2009/oct/20/guardian-quick-carbon-calculator [25th October 2009]

Council of Writing Program Administrators (2003) *Defining and Avoiding Plagiarism: The WPA Statement on Best Practices* available from <http://www.wpacouncil.org/positions/WPAplagiarism.pdf> [10th September 2009]

Elston, C. (2009) Making Group-work Work: An Overview. *Journal of Learning Development in Higher Education* **1**(1): 1–7

Gillett, A., Hammond, A. and Martala, M. (2009) *Successful Academic Writing*. Harlow: Pearson Education

Hacker, D. (2008) *A Writer's Reference with Exercises*. 6th edn. Boston: Bedford/St Martin's

Johns Hopkins University (2009) *Evaluating Information Found on the Internet* available from <http://www.library.jhu.edu/researchhelp/general/evaluating/> [10th September 2009]

National Health Service (2009) *Catch it, Bin it, Kill it*. Coventry: University Hospital

Purdue OWL (2009) *Avoiding Plagiarism* available from <http://owl.english.purdue.edu/owl/resource/589/01/> [10th September 2009]

Purdue OWL (2009) *When Do We Give Credit?* available from <http://owl.english.purdue.edu/owl/resource/589/02/> [10th September 2009]

Skillen, J. (2006) Teaching Academic Writing from the 'Centre' in Australian Universities. In *Teaching Academic Writing in UK Higher Education: Theories, Practices and Models*. Ed. by Ganobcsik-Williams, L. Houndmills: Palgrave Macmillan

INDEX

Note: Page numbers in **bold** are for figures.

GET THE INSIDE TRACK TO ACADEMIC SUCCESS

INSIDE TRACK

SUCCESSFUL ACADEMIC WRITING

ANDY GILLETT, ANGELA HAMMOND & MARY MARTALA

INSIDE TRACK

SUCCEEDING IN EXAMS & ASSESSMENTS

EDDIE BLASS

INSIDE TRACK

WRITING DISSERTATIONS & THESES

NEIL MURRAY & DAVID BEGLAR

Written by a team of highly experienced authors, this series equips students with effective and practical ways to improve their academic skills across all subject areas.